Against the Odds

The survival of Welsh identity

Harold Carter

Sefydliad Materion Cymreig
Institute of Welsh Affairs

The Institute of Welsh Affairs exists to promote quality research and informed debate affecting the cultural, social, political and economic well-being of Wales. IWA is an independent organisation owing no allegiance to any political or economic interest group. Our only interest is in seeing Wales flourish as a country in which to work and live. We are funded by a range of organisations and individuals. For more information about the Institute, its publications, and how to join, either as an individual or corporate supporter, contact:

IWA - Institute of Welsh Affairs
4 Cathedral Road
Cardiff
CF11 9LJ

tel   029 2066 0820
fax   029 2023 3741
email wales@iwa.org.uk
web   www.iwa.org.uk

Contents

Acknowledgements

For help in the writing of this book I would like first to thank my wife, Mari, for such of the understanding of Welsh life I have I owe to her.

My friend and colleague Professor John Aitchison read the manuscript and made valued critical comment.

For the genealogical material in Chapter 1 I am indebted to my nephew, David Carter.

I am especially indebted to John Osmond of the Institute of Welsh Affairs and most particularly to Rhys David for his meticulous and incisive editorial work.

I must add and stress that all the opinions in the book are mine and mine alone.

Harold Carter

Preface

It would seem that a work on Welsh identity is one of supererogation. Daily within the Welsh press there are letters on every aspect of Welshness. Books such as Wyn Griffths' *The Welsh* (1968) are numerous and on Welsh nationalism the numbers are legion. It would appear, therefore, that there is little more that can or indeed need be said. But there are two aspects which demand attention because of their neglect in many discussions. The first of these is the need for clear identification of the bases on which the notion of identity rests. More often than not there is no attempt to demonstrate the criteria on which an argument is developed and assertion takes the place of rational consideration. If one is to try to provide a basis for what constitutes a Welsh identity, it is essential to deconstruct identity into its constituents and to match these to any definition that is proposed.

The second aspect is equally important. It would appear from many discussions in Wales that identity in this Welsh context is seen as unique whereas it is no more than one example in the widest of ranges. Indeed, it is possible to argue that with the ending of the cold war and the fading into the background of confrontation of the super powers what dominates world affairs at present are the conflicts based on perceived identity that have appeared in every part of the world. They are not confined to the West but are active and significant in every continent. The suicide bomber is doing no more than attempting to assert the case for a view which is ethnically based, on the perceived rights of a view of the world which is culturally derived. The Welsh case is therefore just one of many and it is in the context of the many that it should be observed.

This book therefore has these two aspects as its main theme. It seeks to set Welsh identity against a background of the concept of ethnicity and of culture and to relate the Welsh example to contextual situations in the rest of the world.

Chapter 1
A matter of identification

My name is Harold Carter. It would be difficult to devise a name more manifestly English, indeed it is tempting to use the description 'Anglo-Saxon'. Yet, I consider myself as wholly and truly Welsh and I enter that identification in any formal enquiry. Indeed, like others, I wrote 'Welsh' into the 2001 census question on ethnicity where no specific provision for that identity was offered. As a starting point in the consideration of identity it is profitable to pursue how this self-identification has come about. To do that I begin by considering two tables which give my direct line of descent; these are not family trees, only the direct line.

Table 1.1
Harold Carter. Direct Line of descent. Father

John Carter   m   Jane Ann Snowdon
Bapt. 1812,   Bapt. 1816, Gateshead
Newcastle on Tyne
Steam vessel engineer

        |

James Carter   m   Lucy Williams
Born 1836, Gateshead   Born 1835, Swansea
Died Swansea, 1897   Died 1905, Pembrey
Locomotive fireman

        |

Robert Carter   m   Jane (Jenny) Jones
Born 1864, Swansea   Born 1868, Neath
Died 1945, Neath   Died 1931, Neath
Engine driver

        |

Harold Carter   m   Esther Maria Linda Hutchins
Born 1895, Neath   Born 1894, Neath
Died 1963, Neath   Died 1960, Neath
Railway Clerk

        |

Harold Carter
Born 1925, Neath

If Table 1.1 is considered it will be seen that my great, great grandfather was born in Newcastle and married a girl from Gateshead. Their son, James Carter, was born in Gateshead but died in Swansea. He had married a Lucy Williams, who had been born in Swansea. Why the transfer to Swansea took place is not clearly known but the clue possibly lies in the occupation of John Carter as a 'steam vessel engineer'. Family tradition has it that the move was made on the coastal vessels which plied between Newcastle and Swansea. Whether he remained in Swansea because of his marriage or that his marriage is consequent on his staying in Swansea is not known. His occupation as a 'locomotive fireman', however, signals the close family association which developed with the Great Western Railway. The family effectively became distributed along the line with branches in Neath, Llantrisant, Gloucester and Swindon. My grandfather, Robert Carter was born in Swansea and is recorded at the 1901 census as an engine driver but became a member of a breakdown gang for the GWR based in the engine sheds at Penrhiwtyn just outside Neath, where both my father and myself were born. My grandfather, although only one generation removed from Newcastle, was a committed Welshman. A framed portrait of Lloyd George, cut from a newspaper, hung on the wall behind his chair in the kitchen and he was a total supporter of Neath and Wales in rugby.

His wife, Jenny Jones, whom he married in 1883, came from a family originally from Penderyn. She was recorded as a pupil teacher in 1881 and as an assistant school mistress in 1891. According to my father she was Welsh speaking and used the language with her sisters but at the 1901 census she is recorded as speaking English only. My father maintained that her family were founders of a Welsh Congregational Chapel (Annibynwyr) in Melincrythan, part of Neath borough, but that she switched to the Church of England, as it then was, as part of her promotion in teaching. All that is, in itself, a possible reflection of attitudes to the language at the end of the nineteenth century. She never taught my father any Welsh so that he grew up as a monoglot English speaker. That is probably an indication of attitudes to Welsh at that time. My father certainly regarded himself as completely Welsh, however, and always responded angrily to teasing by my wife and myself that one could not be Welsh without speaking the language. But I doubt whether he could have named a single Welsh writer in prose or poetry and his knowledge of history was limited to that of the kings and queens of England and their battles, the traditional material of contemporary historical education in the schools of Wales. Like most working class households of Wales at that time, the house was filled with books. My father read at night to my brother and myself but the books were those such as *Treasure Island*, *Coral Island*, *Tom Brown's Schooldays*, and *Westward Ho!*. There was also, apart from Shakespeare, a wide range of poetry collections, mainly of the nineteenth century romantics. I can recollect his reading to us Masefield's *Reynard the Fox* from the collected poems he had bought. All this was linked to an English cultural milieu, and that of Welsh Wales was completely hidden from him, an unknown, literally a closed book. In brief, his Welsh identity was certainly circumscribed. The only way in which he related to it traditionally is that, though a radical politically, he was more of a Liberal than a full-blooded Socialist.

My mother's family (Table 1.2) can be traced back to Ludgershall in Wiltshire but the family subsequently appears in the neighbourhood of Hungerford in Berkshire. In occupation they seem to vary between being butchers and publicans. Thomas Hutchins, who was baptised in the parish of Chute in 1794, is described as a 'master butcher' in the 1851 census and as a 'Maltster, Brewer and Publican', proprietor of the Wheatsheaf at Chilton Foliat in the 1861 census. Son, William, is an enigma for in the 1851 census he appears in Neath as a butcher and chandler and in the 1861 census as a publican, proprietor of the Queens Hotel in London Road. Why he should have moved to Neath must remain a mystery. The only possibility is that his brother Charles trained as a chemist in London, where he was married in Islington, and subsequently appears as a chemist and druggist at Neath. Perhaps William was encouraged to move by his brother. My maternal grandfather, Alfred Moulding Hutchins, was baptised at Neath in 1861. He married an Agnes Maria Linda Cox who was also born at Neath but whose father and mother were both born in Nailsworth in Gloucestershire. There is thus no Welsh element at all in my mother's line of descent.

Table 1.2
Harold Carter Direct line of descent. Mother

John Hutchence m Ann ?
Bapt. Ludgershall 1683

l

Edward Hutchence m Hannah Lancely
Born Ludgershall   Bapt. 1722
1712

l

Thomas Hutchins m Sarah Stroud
Bapt. Chute 1746   ?

l

Thomas Hutchins m Priscilla Bryant
Bapt. Chute 1794   Bapt. Shalbourne 1795
Maltster, Master Brewer
& Publican

l

William Hutchins m Esther Moulding
Bapt. Chilton Foliat   Bapt. Hungerford 1819
1821
Butcher & Chandler/Publican

l

Alfred Moulding Hutchins m Agnes Maria Linda Cox
Bapt. Neath 1861   Bapt. Neath 1868
Butcher

l

Esther Maria Hutchins m Harold Carter
Born Neath 1894   Born Neath 1895

l

Harold Carter
Born Neath 1925

It is interesting that in the 1891 census Alfred Moulding seems to have described himself as a 'meat purveyor'; a more literal enumerator has overwritten 'butcher'. The 'meat purveyor' suggests the minor pretensions of a tradesman. Indeed, the family, as I remember, was well aware of forebears in the English shires. My mother went to a church school and was confirmed in the Church of England, as it then was. I was at least partly brought up in that tradition and, for example, as in the demands of the Catechism was taught to 'conduct myself humbly and reverently before my betters'! My mother would never tell me how she voted, saying that the ballot was private. That, in a household which was at least Liberal, suggests that she voted Conservative. Having been born in Wales and spent all her life there, she manifestly could not register herself as English but if she had been faced by the demands of the present Labour Force Survey I have no doubt that she would have opted to return herself as 'British'. Here is a type of Welsh identity somewhat different from that of my father. It is that of a person whose whole life, or perhaps a good part, has been spent in Wales but where there is no specific commitment to things Welsh and where all those aspects of being Welsh were merely touched tangentially. A British identity is therefore adopted.

How then do I fit into this inheritance which I have described? My upbringing at Neath was mainly in keeping with my father's character. I thought of myself as Welsh largely through relatively trivial elements such as being a keen supporter of Neath and Wales at rugby, leading to an 'us and them' attitude to things English. My accent was and is unmistakably Welsh. The major transformation took place when I went up to read Geography at the then University College of Wales at Aberystwyth. Aberystwyth claims to be the cultural capital of Wales and certainly I became aware of a much wider and deeper meaning to the notion of Welshness. On my return to college after war service and graduation I was appointed an assistant lecturer in the Department of Geography and Anthropology. Since my research was on Wales, I decided to learn Welsh and went to evening classes but the major influence was my wife, who was a graduate in Welsh and taught Welsh in a number of grammar schools and eventually at Ardwyn Grammar School in Aberystwyth. Her family's first language was Welsh and through that I achieved some ability to speak Welsh, though not with the fluency I would have liked. Even so, a whole new world of literature was opened up and indeed of history. This was the time of a major renaissance in the writing of Welsh history and I was fortunate to count a large number of the academics responsible as friends. My research moved from the field of urban geography to that of the distribution of the Welsh language. I have lectured in Welsh and was invited to give the University of Wales lecture at the Aberystwyth National Eisteddfod. I have been elected an honorary member of the Gorsedd Beirdd Ynys Prydain (the Gorsedd of Bards). In brief, and without further elaboration, I can count myself a Welshman with a total commitment to the culture and language of Wales.

The major point which emerges from this somewhat lengthy review is that here I am as an individual, six out of eight of whose great grandparents were English, born in England, but who now considers himself truly and properly Welsh. A trajectory has led from being strangers in a strange land to complete assimilation. This is surely the right and proper process for in-migrants. Church divines often pontificate on migration and the multiculturalism it produces, but they should look at their own Bible. In the Book of Ruth, Naomi with her husband, Ephraim of Bethlehem Judah, together with their two sons migrate owing to famine into the land of Moab. They are economic migrants. There the husband dies and the two sons marry Moabite women. In due course the two sons die and Naomi decides to return to her native land. Her daughter-in-law Ruth, a Moabitess, insists on returning with her saying, 'Whither thou goest I will go and where thou lodgest I will lodge: thy people shall be my people and thy God my God'. That in many ways defines the attitude incumbent upon migrants. To move into another territory must carry an obligation to accept the way of life of that place, its culture and eventually its identity. Perhaps I can even claim some association here for if 'thy God shall be my God' is an extravagant demand, I can at least claim to have introduced morning service in Gellideg, Capel yr Annibynwyr, my wife's family chapel in Merthyr Tydfil, now alas like so many, defunct.

Two consequences arise from the discussion to this point. The first is that quite unequivocally all the elements of 'Welshness' which I display have been acquired as a member of society and it follows that they have no relation whatsoever to those physical characteristics that are often inappropriately referred to as racial. The colour of one's skin or the dimensions of one's skull have no place at all in the arguments in this book.

The second is that in the course of the analysis of what can be called my ethnic identity I have made reference to a whole series of concepts - culture, ethnicity and identity, for example - and before we can proceed to move from my personal characteristics with which we began into a more general review of 'being Welsh' it is essential to make the analysis a little more formal and to examine these concepts in more detail, for they are the foundations upon which the rest of the argument depends.

Chapter 2
Culture and identity

As soon as the word 'Welsh' is used, either verbally or in written form, two associated problems of definition inescapably arise. The first is a particular one as to what or who constitutes being Welsh and on what criteria does the definition rest. This was the crux of the matter considered in Chapter 1. The second is a generic one. What are the bases of the identification of a number of people as being associated together as a logically constituted group, or a unity of some form, to which a name, such as English, Scots or so on, can be given? The first can for the moment be set aside while the general principles of the generic context are considered.

Political correctness has sadly inhibited discussion of this generic concept. It is symptomatic to have to turn to a journalist to register the restrictions on the straightforward review of ethnic identity. Writing in *The Guardian* (April 20, 2007), Simon Jenkins maintained: 'Anthropology is the most explosive of sciences which is why it keeps its gunpowder hidden. It has more skeletons in its closet, more unmentionables in its past, more hypersensitivity and political delicacy than any other realm of learning. The mere mention of ethnic diversity has academics plugging their ears and slamming paper bags over their heads. The story of group differentiation is so fraught as to render it no-go territory for intellectual research'. As a consequence, a fashionable rush to stress common humanity, led partly by religious pundits, has sidelined those divisions which exist and, paradoxically, contribute to the rich diversity of humankind that is one of its great glories. Perhaps the story of Babel still has its resonances.

Within the diversity noted above, there are two entities. First, there is the nation, a political entity any consideration of which has been bedevilled by association with xenophobia. It is fashionable to condemn the assertion of nationality as something inherently evil. Secondly, within the diversity of peoples, is cultural or ethnic identity, which is somehow conventionally linked with racism, presumably a term derived from 'race', a concept in physical anthropology and related to physical characteristics but which has no relevance whatsoever to notions of culture, way of life or 'ethnie'. Race can therefore be dismissed from this discussion. Also, the concept of the nation state is not the prime concern of this review. But, although it is not necessarily and essentially part of the concept of ethnic identity, it inevitably becomes associated and will therefore have to be considered. Whether distinct ethnic groups should be translated into nation states is a different issue.

Let us return, therefore, to the use of the word 'Welsh' or any other equivalent, keeping the review at this stage on the more general level. Anyone using a word such as Welsh or English or Scots and so on must have some notion of what it signifies in mind. The simplest definition must be that of all the people who live within a demarcated territory but this territorial definition, while having unequivocal meaning, is hardly useful, other than for directly administrative purposes. This is the quantum which the Welsh Assembly has to consider when drawing up its policies for health services and so on but manifestly this universe is ethnically diverse. There are many who live within what is the administrative territory of Wales, as it is at present constituted, who would not consider themselves Welsh, and, indeed, might actively resent being so categorised. If the Office of National Statistics (note the term 'national') were to move its headquarters from London to Newport few of those who shifted with it would be prepared immediately to categorise themselves as Welsh. Conversely, there are many living outside the administrative territory of Wales who *would* regard themselves as 'being Welsh'.

One way of avoiding this dilemma is to invent hybrid categories, such as British-Asian, or the more widely used Afro-American, although the vast bulk of those so identified have not the slightest relation to any African culture or way of life. But it does point toward a different concept which has no direct relation to territory but is rather related to the categorisation of self, to attitude of mind. So a new definition is needed and a much more tendentious field, perhaps a thicket would be a better metaphor, is opened up. For the idea that self-identification, a 'them and us' contrast, offers a solution is illusory since the criteria on which such decisions are made themselves have to be defined and the whole complex question of the criteria for identity is reopened. There is no simple way forward, therefore, other than to consider a formal definition of culture or ethnicity, for the two relate to the same concept.

As long ago as 1952 two American anthropologists attempted to review the widest range of definitions of culture. They assembled some 158 definitions under eight broad headings – descriptive or enumerative, historical, normative, psychological, structural, genetic, and a last group termed 'incomplete'. To this assemblage they added their own definition as a summation of their review: 'Culture consists of patterns, explicit and implicit, of and for behaviour acquired and transmitted by symbols, constituting the distinctive achievement of human groups, including their embodiment in artefacts; the essential core of culture consists of traditional (i.e. historically derived and selected) ideas and especially their attached values: culture systems may, on the one hand, be considered as products of action, on the other as conditioning influences upon further action' (Kroeber and Kluckhohn, 1952, 181). To this can be added a definition of ethnicity from Wikipedia, not perhaps the most reliable of sources but one which provides a reasoned interpretation. 'An ethnic group or ethnicity is a population of human beings whose members identify with each other, usually on the basis of a presumed common genealogy or ancestry. Recognition by others as a distinct ethnic group is often a contributory factor to developing this bond of identification. Ethnic groups are often united by common cultural, behavioural, linguistic, ritualistic or religious traits' (Wikipedia, 2007).

Before considering these definitions in greater detail, there are two aspects which need immediate clarification. The first is implicit in Kroeber and Kluckhohn's definition. Cultural character is not determined once and for all; it is not the dead hand of the past. There is constant change and modification with time. To stress this was the intention of Gwyn A. Williams in '*When Was Wales?*' (Williams, 1979). Those characteristics which may define what is Welshness in 2008 will be greatly different from those appropriate in 1908. One may well search for the unchanging and the permanent but there is no certainty that it will be found. Foremost among the significant causes of change are forces impinging from outside the culture, so that every culture is in the process of adapting to or rejecting external pressures. It is this process which becomes most controversial as the immigration of 'outsiders' leads to modification from a perceived ideal or established condition. To put the issue at its crudest, should sharia law have any part to play in a British way of life as a consequence of Muslim immigration? This is an issue which will have to be considered later.

The second aspect which needs discussion is that of scale. Levi-Strauss in his attempt at defining culture wrote, 'What is called culture is a fragment of humanity which, from the point of view of the research at hand and of the scale on which the latter is carried out, presents significant discontinuities in relation to the rest of humanity......Since these discontinuities may be reduced to invariants, which is the goal of structural analysis, we see that culture may, at the same time, correspond to objective reality and be a function of the kind of research undertaken. Accordingly, the same set of individuals may be considered to be parts of many different cultural contexts, universal, continental, national, regional, local etc., as well as familial, occupational, religious, political etc. This is true as a limit; however anthropologists usually reserve the term "culture" to designate a group of discontinuities which is significant on several of these levels at the same time. That it can never be valid for all levels does not prevent the concept of culture being fundamental for the anthropologist' (Levi-Strauss, 1968, 295).

Perhaps the best illustration of the above statement in relation to Wales is the stereotype of the south Wales valleys in the heyday of the coal mining industry. What was derived from part of south Wales was extended to become characteristic of the whole of Wales regardless of the fact that it was totally inappropriate for the country as a whole. Indeed, it could well be maintained that the defining characteristics of the 'Valleys' are not in themselves specifically 'Welsh', but rather relate to mining communities, that is to an occupational group as noted by Levi-Strauss above. Thus, parallel communities in the north of England display the same qualities, closely knit, Nonconformist with a choral tradition and an addiction to rugby, albeit Rugby League rather than Rugby Union. What was distinctive about the south Welsh valley communities was the Welsh language, which linked these peoples to the literary and other traditions of Wales. But the growth of Socialism brought with it an internationalism whereby the unity of the 'workers of the world' became a predominant theme. In the end the mining communities sacrificed much of their specifically Welsh inheritance and hence arose the continuing and at times quite bitter antagonisms between Labour and Plaid Cymru, in spite of the fact that they both claim to be Socialist in principle.

In the discussion of the nature of culture which follows, therefore, two factors must be borne in mind. Cultures are dynamic, they change and are modified over time, and scale is crucial and needs to be specified. At least some Welsh people as they react to scale would opt for a series that goes from Wales direct to the European Union, while others would opt for the intermediate position as British. With these reservations in mind it is possible to take forward the definitions that have been adduced by a consideration of the most fundamental elements which dominate in the creation of an ethnic identity. Among these language and religion appear to be paramount.

'The importance of your learning – and conforming to – the rules spelled out, entry by entry, in *The Official Politically Correct Dictionary and Handbook* cannot be overemphasised. For as linguists Edward Sapir and Benjamin Wharf suspected as early as the 1940s – and postmodernist theory has confirmed – language is not merely the mirror of society, it is the major force in "constructing" what we perceive as "reality" ' (Beard and Cerf, 1992, xiii).

It might seem odd to begin a consideration of language with a quotation from such a source but it illustrates the fundamental significance of language as a basis for the interpretation of the surrounding environment. Beard and Cerf, indeed, preface their work with a reference to George Orwell's *1984* – 'It was intended that when Newspeak had been adopted once and for all and Oldspeak forgotten, a heretical thought...should be literally unthinkable, at least in so far as thought depended on words'.

The attempt to impose a politically correct vocabulary, the Sapir-Wharf hypothesis and Orwell's Newspeak are all expressions of the same contention, that the language people speak profoundly shapes the way in which they think and act. As Mandlebaum has observed:

'Human beings do not live in the objective world alone, nor alone in the world of social activity as ordinarily understood but are very much at the mercy of the particular language which has become the medium of expression for the society. It is quite an illusion to imagine that one adjusts to reality essentially without the use of language and language is merely an incidental means of solving problems of communication and reflection.' (Mandelbaum, 1949,162).

Postmodernism is obsessed with iconography and semiotics, that is with the significance of signs and symbols, all the modes of perception and expression of the environment in which people live and have their being. All these are deeply ritualised and conditioned by language. To quote from an interpretation of the cultural anthropology of Mary Douglas:

'Ritual carries or transmits collective information, like language. But it is also true that language acts like a ritual, and its structures – its codes – are part of society's arsenal of ritual utilised in the periodic affirmation and reproduction of basic social relations and commonly held values' (Wuthnow,1984,104).

At this point another extensive quotation from the work of Anthony D. Smith can be introduced. Seeking to define ethnicity he writes:

> 'It relates mainly to a sense of community based on history and culture, rather than to any collectivity or to the concept of ideology. In this, I follow the emendation proposed by Epstein to the literature of "situational" ethnicity in which the growth of a sense of the collective self is treated as an important part of a group (especially ethnic) identity and solidarity. Only here, the sense of self is viewed through the prism of symbol and mythologies of the community's heritage....The core of ethnicity, as it has been transmitted in the historical record and as it shapes individual experience, resides in this quartet of "myths, memories, values and symbols" and the characteristic forms or styles and genres of certain historical configurations of populations' (Smith, 1986, 14/15).'

But these myths, memories values and symbols are all acquired through language. 'Different speech systems or codes create for their speakers different orders of relevance. The experience of the speakers may then be transformed by what is made significant or relevant by different speech systems....The social structure becomes in this way the sub-stratum of the child's experience essentially through the manifold consequences of the linguistic processes. From this point of view, every time the child speaks or listens the social structure is reinforced in him and his social identity shaped' (Bernstein, 1970, 124).'

The conclusion from this brief discussion is evident. Language is a prime component in defining identity. This can be taken even further since accent, too, within a language can identify sub-groups. To take myself as an example, I have only to speak a few words in English before being identified as Welsh, and further as south Welsh. Indeed, a Professor Higgins could locate my birthplace to within Swansea Bay. But perhaps the best example of the significance of language comes from the Book of Judges. After the men of Gilead under Jephthah had defeated the Ephraimites those of that people who had escaped attempted to cross the Jordan. But the men of Gilead well knew how to identify an enemy, someone of another ethnic group. ... 'Then the men of Gilead said unto him "Art thou an Ephraimite?" If he said "Nay", then they said unto him, "Say now Shibboleth": and he said "Sibboleth": for he could not frame to pronounce it right. Then they took him, and slew him at the passage of the Jordan: and there fell at that time of the Ephraimites forty and two thousand'. Language discriminates: language defines identity.

It is interesting to add the contemporary impact of Spanish in the USA brought about by immigration from Latin America, especially Mexico. The result has been a threat to American English as the only official language, one of the hallmarks of American identity. In response, a number of states have passed measures to register English as the only official language. Significantly, among these are the states most threatened. California made English the official language in 1986 by a majority of 73 per cent and Florida by 85.5 per cent in 1988.

This discussion on language has been on the very general scale but it is worthwhile bringing it down to the individual level. The author, Sathnam Sanghera, has written about his own experience in his book *'If You Don't Know Me by Now'*. Commenting on his experience in relation to the proposal by Lord Goldsmith in 2008 that there should be some sort of loyalty oath for teenagers, he writes of his family, 'We lived in Britain, but in many ways we were actually Punjabi villagers. There were no knives and forks in the house. Our lives were governed by the Sikh religion and Indian superstition. Our parents did not speak English.' But, he says he and others have grown up to be active and proud British citizens, with jobs and a sense off belonging. 'Did inspired teachers force us to swear daily American-style pledges besides the British flag, our brown turmeric-stained hands placed over our hearts? Did Wolverhampton City Council set aside a British "national day"? Were we injected with HP sauce and forced to sing *Jerusalem* until we gave in? No, it was more simple than that, we learned English.....'(Sanghera, 2008). It would be crass to add anything to that.

At the outset we noted that this discussion was not specifically concerned with nationhood, that is with the relation between 'ethnie' and independent national status. Even so, it is necessary at least to note the role of language in that context. Belgium has consistently demonstrated the possibility of breaking into French-speaking (Walloon) and Flemish-speaking parts. Quebec, in Canada, has just as consistently manifested a demand for separation - 'Vivre Quebec Libre' à la President De Gaulle. Examples are manifold of the role of language in irredentist movements.

If the world is perceived through the medium of language, it has been in large part interpreted through religion. For this analysis the truth or untruth of belief is irrelevant as is the anthropological discussion of the origins of religion. What matters in terms of ethnic identity is simply the belief system and the consequences it engenders. These consequences are self evident, as for example in the 'troubles' in Ulster or in the disasters at the time of the division of imperial India into contemporary India and Pakistan when the withdrawal of the British 'raj' led to a death toll which makes that of the Ephraimites seem trivial.

In many ways religion is a more obviously perceived basis of difference between population groups, accompanied as it so often is by a rich range of visual symbols - the Cross, images of the Madonna or icons of various sorts are obvious examples. Even in those religions where the representation of 'graven images' is forbidden other symbols are clearly evident, for example in the burkha, or the Sikh headdress or the Kara. Also, religious beliefs are given physical visibility. Christmas and Easter by their role in the calendar control the tenor of life in western cultures, though it is interesting and significant to note that in Britain Whitsun has disappeared in favour of a secular holiday. It is also symptomatic that some local authorities in England attempt to pander to multiculturalism by either outlawing these Christian festivals or substituting some anodyne replacement.

Even further, the human body itself is subject to the calls of religion. Male circumcision is the obvious example but whereas it arouses little controversy female circumcision does, for it creates the greatest of antagonisms between cultures. Indeed, the treatment of young girls becomes a point of conflagration, exacerbating the basic differences derived from belief systems. Here lies one of the major problems where toleration vanishes and one culture describes the usages of another as totally unacceptable. In The Times (March 14, 2008) Margaret Moran, a Labour member of the Commons Home Affairs Select Committee, commenting on arranged or forced marriages in some Asian communities is recorded as saying, 'This can involve violence, rape, kidnap – what more important issue can there be? The cultural thing is just a big smokescreen'. It is a paradox that those who are most vociferous in the promotion of multiculturalism often take the leading role in condemning practices that do not conform to their own behavioural, that is cultural, systems. It is perhaps worth recording that unacceptable practices are condemned as barbaric, a term itself originally derived from a cultural distinction based on language.

Religion thus becomes a major element of ethnic differentiation precisely because the customs of one group are inimical to those of another, or at least are regarded as strange and incomprehensible. Dietary customs are a good example. In illustration, Mary Douglas (Douglas, 2003) uses the example of Eleazar in Maccabees (2,vi,18). The eating of pork by the Jews became a symbol of submission to Antiochus who had conquered Israel. Eleazar refused to eat pork and was in consequence executed. Douglas points out that there was no fundamental issue to the conqueror in the eating of pork but it had become a symbol of difference, of allegiance, all the more so because of its meaningless to other cultures. But perhaps the best known example is the crisis engendered by the use of animal fats by the British in India to grease the cartridges in the guns issued to sepoys and the role it played in the Indian Mutiny or, as it is called in India, the First War of Independence. Those two names stress how cultural conflicts are translated into political terms.

All these symbols are manifestations of those fundamental distinctions which are lodged within ethnic groups and serve to stress difference. They are derived from customs and usages unique to the groups. The treatment of women is one sphere which has already been introduced in relation to the mutilation of the body. In Islam women are more clearly seen as set apart from males, possibly inferior in status, and liable to sets of controls. The whole structure of houses is designed to facilitate seclusion. High external walls with but small entrances characterise domestic architecture. That seclusion is carried to the outside world in the use of the burkha, effectively the confining walls of the residence made mobile. Whereas seclusion and all its attendant facets create no problem when confined to the core areas of Islam, carried to cultures with very different ways they immediately create antagonisms. The determination of marriage partner by family rather than by the individual and the insistence of marriage within religious groups, and the so-called honour killings which result from its flouting, all illustrate the totally different ways of living within ethnic groups consequent upon religious belief. A simple example that has given rise to a great deal of anger is whether a Moslem living in Britain should be able to have two wives, for clearly within the laws of Britain it is bigamy. Whether the customs of an immigrant group should be allowed to stand outside the law of the land is a question that the

Archbishop of Canterbury posed to considerable controversy in 2008. In this same vein, even within general belief systems there can be significant and serious differences. Within the early church Arianism and other heresies were rooted out with violence. The differences between Protestant and Roman Catholic in Northern Ireland is an obvious and tragic example.

Secularisation has greatly reduced the impact of older religious custom and convention in many parts of the world, especially in the West, but, as apparent from the discussion above, it has made conflict with more conservative elements all the more inflammatory. Turkey is a clear example, where the fear that the secular state, established by Kemal Attaturk in the early years of the 20th century, will be transformed back into an Islamised state is at present the subject of conflict. Abdullah Gul, elected president in 2008, is a member of the mildly Islamic Justice and Development AK Party. This has aroused strong concerns that through his presidency the secular basis of the state is being undermined. Significantly, the conflict has become polarised over the wearing of the headscarf by women. His wife, Hayrunisa Gul, commonly wears the scarf and the wearing of the scarf by students on campus, which was forbidden in the determination to preserve secularism, has become the centre of the conflict between different views of the role of religion in everyday life. Religious symbols matter.

The traditions which identify ethnic groups reach beyond the two main bases of language and religion and can be summarised as myths, memories and values. Diet has long been a mark of distinction, in part derived from religion, as noted above. Beyond that, the French have traditionally referred to the English as 'Rosbifs; the English have referred to the French as 'Frogs' and the Germans as 'Krauts'. Such terminology has long become unacceptable in an era of political correctness.

Recently the impact of immigration has led to the identifying characteristics of Englishness being widely debated, as in Jeremy Paxman's somewhat discursive book (*The English. A Portrait of a People, 1998*). Language, in this instance is of course no measure since English has become a well nigh universal tongue, even if accents vary. At the same time the Church of England, which was once the dominant institution in religious belief and, indeed, at the heart of the social system, has long lost its pre-eminence. Even Protestant Christianity in a broader sense can no longer be regarded as an identifier in what has become a secular society but at the same time much of the way of life looked upon as characteristically English has been derived from the rites and traditions of the Church. And the Church of England still retains its role in 'national occasions', such as coronations, even though the future king, Prince Charles, wants to identify himself as a 'defender of the faiths', rather than of *the* faith.

One of the problems is that the vital myths and memories of the English people predominantly relate to its imperial past and have become in some cases a matter for penitence; for apology, rather than celebration. The true England only emerges on rare occasions when the reins of what is deemed acceptable are relaxed, such as the last night of the BBC Promenade Concerts. It is ironic that the glories of imperial Rome, one of the bloodiest and cruellest of empires, are celebrated by the academic establishment while those of imperial England are hidden in a sense of shame. Here lies the problem of being 'English' and of being at the same time politically correct and 'liberal'.

A much more robust defence of basic identifying values has been set out by Samuel P. Huntington in his book, *'Who are We? America's Great Debate'*. He identifies an 'American Creed', as initially formulated by Thomas Jefferson and elaborated by many others, and 'widely viewed as the crucial defining element of American identity. The creed was, however, the product of the distinct Anglo-Protestant culture of the founding settlers of America.....Key elements of that culture include: the English language; Christianity; religious commitment; English concepts of the rule of law, the responsibility of rulers and the rights of individuals; and dissenting Protestant values of individualism, the work ethic, and belief that humans have the ability and duty to try to create a heaven on earth'. (Huntington, 2004, xvi). The bulk of Huntington's book is devoted to the support of these features of the creed against all the diverse cultural streams that have entered the USA in more recent times and against the fashionable theme of multiculturalism. Huntington's definition of the creed is surely no more than an assemblage of the myths, memories, values and symbols that have been derived from the early history of the United States.

Every ethnic group creates the myths upon which it rests its identity. Certainly, the most potent of the Welsh myths is that of Owain Glyn Dŵr – *Y Mab Darogan*. Elissa R. Henken in her book *'National Redeemer. Owain Glyndŵr in Welsh Tradition'* (1996) demonstrates a whole gamut of ways in which the redeemer hero has been and is represented as a symbol of identity. Perhaps the drowning of the village of Capel Celyn and the creation of Llyn Celyn constitutes a more recent myth: *Cofia Dryweryn*.

As the above implies, most myths are derived from actual events which have become raised in status and lodged in memory. One of the more potent and deep seated of Irish myths is that of the great famine of the 1840s ascribed to English exploitation and inhumanity. Perhaps an even better example is given by Micheal O Siochru in his book on Oliver Cromwell's Irish expeditions (O Siochru, 2008). The Irish prime minister, Bertie Ahern, was paying a courtesy visit to the British foreign secretary, Robin Cook, in 1997 when he noticed a painting of Oliver Cromwell in the room. He walked out and refused to return until the portrait of 'that murdering bastard' was removed. It matters not how valid interpretations are but that the events of the period have become fixed in folk memory and by that turned into the basis of an identity symbol. Even place names become part of the process. Zimbabwe and Harare replaced Southern Rhodesia and Salisbury. Significantly, a name had to be invented for a political entity that was the creation of a colonial regime. The result was the adoption of a name from a ninth century culture, probably of the San people, which had little relation to the subsequent Bantu invaders who make up the bulk of the present population. Zimbabwe is an apt illustration of the search for myths in the search for identity.

The situation in South Africa is particularly fascinating as so many of the country's place names are derived from the heroes of the Voortrek, the migration of the Boers into the heart of southern Africa. The prime example is Pretoria, the centre of government, which bears the name of Andries Pretorius on a site chosen in 1854 by his son, Marthinus Pretorius, to be the capital of the Transvaal. There are demands that the name should be changed into one more in keeping with the new rainbow nation. Interestingly, because of the emphasis on the so-called rainbow *nation*, names have to be more in keeping with that entity, rather than the various ethnic groups out of which it was created. Conflict has arisen in Durban, too, over the attempt of the ANC to rename streets that carry the names of white settlers with those of ANC and Marxist activists.

It follows from this brief survey that although the prime identifiers of ethnicity are language and religion, there exists a whole mélange of other criteria which act as reinforcers. Many of these are intangible, difficult to isolate and define, but make up for each group what Huntington calls the 'creed', that complex which makes a group feel different and independent from fellow human beings. Paxman's book is an attempt to establish a 'creed' for the English. Indeed, where no symbols exist they are often invented. Many of the symbols of Scottish identity - the tartans, the kilt and the pipes - were created in the nineteenth century.

There is a further realm in which a people's identity is lodged and for which it is unfortunate that the term 'culture' has to be used, not in its anthropological sense but with its more general meaning. As such, a division can be made into 'high culture' and 'folk culture'. High culture primarily embraces the whole range of the arts, literature and drama, music and all the visual arts. Together, they are taken to represent 'the distinct achievement of human groups' to quote from a definition given earlier in this chapter, and that achievement is accordingly celebrated and becomes an element of distinction. One obvious example is Burns Night, an expression of the identity of the Scots. In the whole panoply of English literature the works of Shakespeare are most often taken as the representative of an extensive body of literature that sets the English apart.

There are, however, two problems with high culture as a distinguishing element. The first is that the most widely acclaimed work becomes universal in its appeal. It is hardly possible to see Mozart as somehow being used as a key to German or Austrian identity. By becoming universal the crucial limitation to and identification with one group is lost; even Wagner with all the associations of his music is still of universal significance. The second problem is that high culture tends to be limited in its appeal to a small section of the population, to an elite. A recent survey claimed that the most popular poet in England is T. S. Eliot, an American by birth. It would be interesting to ascertain in a random sample of the population of, say, Liverpool how many could quote just a single line of Eliot's work, even given the popularity of the musical based on his work, 'Cats'. It is worth considering here the work of Welsh art critic and cultural commentator, Peter Lord. With quite magnificent zeal and scholarship he has virtually single-handedly established the existence of a significant line of Welsh art. But important as it is to a limited band of scholars, it can hardly be seen in more general terms as solidifying the identity of the Welsh either to Welsh people themselves or the outside world in general.

Set against the constraints on high culture it would seem at first that folk culture, representing as it does the customs and usages of the common people, would be a more viable element of definition. Here, too, problems arise. Industrialisation, which has seen the displacement of rural traditions and the diminution of the significance of distance, has meant that older customs have either disappeared or been significantly modified to become well-nigh universal rather than local. Mothering Sunday, once part of the church calendar, has become Mothers' Day and All Saints has given way to Halloween. Universal materialism has displaced local festivals. For modern purposes it is possible to translate folk culture into popular culture but here too globalisation has undermined what once could be called 'ethnic'. Pop groups seek not to epitomise the local but to gain maximum exposure and maximum profits on the world market. The very term 'ethnic' is now used for the artefacts from the developing world where some relation to locality still pertains.

Perhaps within popular culture it is in sport that an association with locality remains, or rather has been more recently developed to replace older customs. National teams and individuals, and here one has to use the word national for it is in that guise they appear, have become cores of expressed identity, even to the extent of violence. There is little point in following this well known phenomenon at any length but to Welsh people one movement will be of interest and is an effective exemplar. The Catalans have begun to demand that they should field an international soccer team as distinct from their inclusion in Spain. The precedent quoted is, of course, the position of Wales, Scotland and Northern Ireland.

One final set of bases of identity needs to be considered and that is made up of the institutions that groups set up or recognise as markers of their separation. At this point, of course, discussion most nearly impinges on the concept of the nation, which presumably implies a more formal recognition of identity, primarily, though not necessarily, political in nature. The problem of English identity was earlier broached but it is most manifestly displayed in its set of institutions, including, for example, the monarchy and parliament, each made apparent in associated buildings, Buckingham Palace and the Houses of Parliament, just as the rule of law is symbolised in the Law Courts. Over the Palace flies the Royal Standard. Other buildings display the Cross of St George, greatly deployed in recent times as a mark of the English. Flags and banners are potent symbols, hence the regularity with which they are burned by the disaffected. This brief comment on institutions will be extended at a later stage.

This chapter has attempted to translate into a more formal context the personal narrative of the first chapter, to present some of the criteria by which ethnic identity is defined. But the populations defined by these criteria do not exist in vacuo. They are strongly related to territory. It is necessary to give to these populations 'a local habitation and a name'.

Chapter 3

Identity and territory

God gave all men all earth to love,
But, since our hearts are small,
Ordained for each one spot should prove
Beloved over all...
(Rudyard Kipling)

At first in a study of Wales it would seem that a consideration of identity and territory is unnecessary. After all, apart from the anomaly that until the administrative reorganisation of 1974 the term Wales and Monmouthshire was sometimes used, the territory of Wales has been fixed for nearly four hundred years. Even so, W. T. R. Pryce (2006) has demonstrated how frequently both English geographers and planners have ignored the Welsh frontier in drawing up 'regions' of the United Kingdom. He writes, 'we have … reviewed some of the approaches of outsiders who, from time to time, looked at Wales in the light of an agenda that, in reality, did not recognise the national integrity of the country (Pryce, 2006, 151). There are many occasions when that same integrity is ignored. Welsh Water only covers part of Wales, the rest coming under its Severn Trent counterpart. Postal regions cross the border, Shrewsbury serving the whole of Mid Wales. There is a Transport Commissioner for Wales…and the Midlands located at Birmingham. In another context, there may be some dirigistes along the border who would welcome a transfer to England, and certainly, in complete contrast, a goodly number who would like to change what is no more than a provincial boundary into a truly national one. But these are minor issues, and objectors, with very minor exceptions, work through constitutional means. Across the world, however, this same matter of territory has been the very core of problems related to identity and it needs to be reviewed if only to show what, at least in modern times, Wales has avoided. For, as we shall demonstrate, in earlier times this too was a Welsh problem.

The most obvious examples of what can be called 'territoriality' are found at the smallest of scales. The gangs that are found in large cities are in reality cultural groups. They often have their own language, although argot is the better term; certainly they have distinctive dress codes and rituals associated with initiation and behaviour. Especially, they have their own territory, or turf, often marked out by graffiti (Ley and Cybriwsky, 1974), rather as a tomcat sprays to define its area. In contemporary London these territories apparently correspond with post codes. Infringement of these territories is viewed as a challenge and can lead to violence; much of the knife crime of present day British cities is related to such infringement.

In a sad parallel much of the world's violence and bloodshed is derived from the conflicting territorial interests of ethnic groups. The terms ethnic cleansing and genocide have become all too familiar in modern times. As these ethnic characteristics are expressed in territory, the context of discussion does change from that of the ethnic group to that of the nation, for in many ways the spatial expression of ethnicity is the nation, primarily a spatial concept. With that in mind, the territorial disputes which now become the theme of this chapter can be put into a number of different categories.

The first of these is the dispute over territory by rival claimants. The spatial boundaries of any culture are seldom well-defined; characteristically they diminish outward from a dominant core to an attenuated fringe where overlap with others occurs. As a result, at the margins conflict with neighbours arises. This becomes especially problematic if the area so concerned has some significant meaning to either side. The second situation is the containment of an ethnic group within a larger territory. This is classic irredentism where a distinctive group contained within a controlling political entity seeks to gain 'independence'. Independence movements have been apparent over the whole of human history and still remain a major cause of conflict. The standard expression is, of course, in nationalisms.

Closely associated, but possibly somewhat different is the condition of those ethnic groups that have been perforce associated within one polity by the operation of external power. Most characteristic are the nations of Africa, which to a great extent were the creations of colonial powers, and where boundaries bear little or no relation to long standing tribal identities. Inter-tribal problems have been the consequence. The fourth situation is where either through conquest or by immigration an alien group has been inserted into the territory of another and where a section of space is effectively appropriated.

These various conditions will appear in the chapters that follow but at this stage a brief exemplification can be presented. The most obvious example of a clash over territory is that between Israel and the Palestinians. Let me state that the purpose here is not to present a balanced view of an Israeli-Palestinian conflict, rather the opposite. For the purpose here is to demonstrate how the claims to territory of an ethnic population arise. Also at this point it is necessary to note that at least to some scholars the facts of the early history of the Jews are open to question. There very little archaeological evidence to support the Old Testament as history (Cline, 2009); and Shlomo Sand in his book '*The Invention of the Jewish People* (2009) dismisses most of the Biblical narrative as myth. From our point of view this is of no consequence. Identity depends largely on myth and its acceptance makes it reality.

The Hebrews seem to have been a group of pastoral nomads who about the end of the second century BC migrated under the leadership of Abraham from Mesopotamia in search of the land promised to them by Yahweh. 'Get thee out of thy country and from thy kindred and from thy father's house, unto a land that I will shew thee' (Genesis, 12, 1). 'And I will give unto thee and to thy seed after thee the land wherein thou art a stranger, all the land of Canaan, for an everlasting possession; and I will be thy God' (Genesis, 12 ,17). They followed the lands of the Fertile Crescent into Canaan, into the upland plateaux of what is now Palestine. From thence they wandered south, presumably driven by drought, and eventually settled in Egypt, in the land of Goshen which lies in the east of the Nile Delta. But when there arose in Egypt 'a man who knew not Joseph', the descendant of Abraham, the Israelites were turned into slaves and hence came about their exodus under Moses.

It is under Moses in their trek north that a covenant with Yahweh is made and Moses is given on Mount Sinai the laws by which they must live, inscribed on the tablets enshrined in the Ark of the Covenant. Along with the commandments go the whole series of rites and rituals gathered together in the book of Leviticus, for they were probably accumulated over a long period rather than solely under Moses. Moses leads them to Canaan, the Promised Land. 'This is the land that I swore unto Abraham, unto Isaac, and unto Jacob, saying I will give it unto thy seed; I have caused thee to see it with thine eyes but thou shalt not go over thither' (Deuteronomy, 34, 4). It is left to Joshua therefore to lead the Israelites to the forceful occupation of this their new, settled homeland, although at no point do they seem to have been in what can be called sole occupation. Joshua then apportions the land between the twelve tribes. To this point, and the occupation seems to date to about 1240 BC, the people form a loose federation and it is not until much later under David that they are united into what can be called a political entity with the organs of a state, a civil service and an army. Above all, under David, the Jebusite fortress of Jerusalem is captured and turned into the capital city where the Temple is built and where the Ark is lodged. Thus, a significant and lasting symbol of Israel is established.

Gwyn Rowley, who writes with insight into Arab-Israeli relations has proposed a basic triad at the root of Israeli identity symbolising the intimate relationship between God, the people and the land. God stands as the epitome of the beliefs, rites and rituals which form the culture of the chosen people, the ethnic group, which occupied the sacred territory given to them by God. As Rowley summarises, 'No real understanding of the development of Israel can be forthcoming without an appreciation of the impact of the covenant of land on a lost, displaced, afraid and homeless people, wandering in a wilderness (Rowley, 1984, 5).

We have established the significance of the territory to the ethnic group, an essential element of its being. To trace the subsequent history of the Jews is beyond the scope of this brief survey. Situated as they were at the heart of the lines of movement between Mesopotamia and Egypt, they were overrun by a succession of empires, from the Assyrians and the Persians to the Greeks and the Romans. It was under the Romans that the refusal to accept subservience led to the destruction of the Temple, and with the apocalyptic stand at Masada, to final dispersion, the Diaspora. The area was renamed Palestina by the Romans in an attempt to eradicate the possibility of any Jewish resurgence. It remained under the Eastern Empire until the coming of Islam and, eventually, control under another imperial system, that of the Ottoman Turks.

It was with the collapse of the Ottoman Empire after the First World War that the present problems began. The anti-Semitism present in Europe as well as the pogroms of the nineteenth and early twentieth centuries led to the promise of a national home for the Jews in the Balfour Declaration of 1917. After the war Britain was given a mandate over Palestine and it was during this period that Jewish terrorism, 'one man's terrorist is another's freedom fighter', promoted the cause of Zionism. Britain relinquished the mandate in 1948 and 'on the day the British withdrew, the Jewish national provincial council at Tel Aviv unilaterally proclaimed the new state of Israel. Fighting broke out immediately between the Arab and Jewish factions. The better armed and organised Jewish forces, with the resources and influence of international Zionism, occupied not only the territory allotted to the Jewish state, as envisaged by the United Nations, but also more than half of that earmarked for the proposed Arab state' (Rowley, 1984, 26-7). Ultimately, the attempt by the Arab states to defeat and eliminate Israel in the Six Day War of 1967 led to the Israeli occupation of the West Bank, East Jerusalem, the Gaza Strip and the Golan Heights, the situation as at the time of writing apart from the return of the Gaza Strip. The land given by God was once again in Jewish hands. The consequence was the building on the western bank of a whole series of Israeli settlements, on land the UN had assigned to the Palestinians. It was in this way that the conflict over territory between Israel and the Palestinians was engendered. Within Israel conflict, too, developed between extreme Zionists, for whom the land had been given by God as a sacred trust, and pragmatists willing to sacrifice the land in return for peace and security.

As I stated earlier, this is certainly not the place to look for some resolution; that is not the purpose of the review we have carried out, which has been intentionally developed entirely from the Israeli viewpoint. What the survey has done is to emphasise the significance of land, of territory in the context of ethnic identity. Rowley's interpretation of the Israeli linkage of culture, or way of life, people and land can be made more general for there is a universal association of those three elements. It can be illustrated by another example.

Kosovo, like Palestine, illustrates the way in which extreme violence results from the clash of ethnic groups over territory and indeed introduces that ugly term, ethnic cleansing, which had been first used in the Balkans in connection with the Serb massacres in Bosnia. There is no need to follow at length the extremely complex history of Kosovo. Briefly, it was part of medieval Serbia between 1180 and 1455 when it was taken over by the expanding Turkish Empire. But that expansion had been fervently resisted by the Serbs and their heroic resistance at the Battle of Kosovo, the Field of the Blackbirds, in 1389 became part of Serbian mythology, celebrated in poetry as a heroic defeat and a symbol of their past greatness. 'The legend of Kosovo has grown gradually. It was inspired by the belief that the Battle of Kosovo was the greatest tragedy the Serbs had had to face. It was the end of their medieval greatness, the end of their freedom for five hundred years. The Kosovo *pesme* (heroic verses) are Homeric in simplicity and grandeur. Against overwhelming odds Stephen Lazar makes the choice not to accept Turkish vassaldom without fighting and this has become a prototype for the Serbian people....And so Kosovo and all it symbolises has grown into a cult' (Naval Intelligence Division, 1944, Yugoslavia, Vol. 2, 306). But under the Turks some Islamisation took place and conflict was generated between Kosovo and the neighbouring and ethnically different Albania, where, after centuries of isolation under the Turks, some seventy per cent were Moslems. After the First World War Kosovo became part of Yugoslavia but during the Second World War with the disruption in that country thousands of Serbs in Kosovo were either killed or expelled by Albanians.

Under the totalitarian rule of Marshall Tito, the Yugoslav leader, ethnic conflict was strictly controlled but with his going it rapidly broke out and a now independent Serbia took steps to retain Kosovo as part of what was dreamed of as a greater Serbia. Between 1995 and 1999 armed conflict ensued between Serbia and the Kosovo Liberation Army that had been formed in 1982. Serbia was accused, under President Slobodan Milosevic in particular, of operating a system of ethnic cleansing. In 1999 Nato intervened, bombing targets in Serbia, leading to a ceasefire at the Kumanovo Agreement in 1999 when Kosovo came under UN control. Eventually in 2008, after a referendum, Kosovo now dominated by ethnic Albanians, became an independent country. But the Serbs still refuse to recognise that independence, for to them it is part of their historic past, not exactly a sacred territory but one at the very heart of their identity as a people. Here again is a story of conflict and bloodshed as the determination of ethnic groups to retain territory associated with their very being is defended. In more recent times, with the capture of former Bosnian Serb leader, Radovan Karadzic, and a government more concerned with membership of the European Union than with its past, there is every possibility that these conflicts will be resolved, although to some Serbs this will be the sacrifice of a cultural inheritance for a mess of EU pottage. Another long lasting and well known example of conflict over territory is Kashmir where a line of control, a frontier, established after a war between India and Pakistan in 1948 has failed to contain the ambitions of both but especially of the Muslims within the Indian held part.

The second condition which we suggested is the containment of an ethnic minority within the confines of a larger territorial unit. The term territorial unit is a euphemism for what in nearly all cases is a state. Inevitably, we are here concerned with ethnic groups viewed as nations. This is probably the most common of all conflicts over territory and is evident in all parts of the world, marked in some cases by extreme violence. In September 2008 war flared briefly in the Caucasus as South Ossetia attempted to free itself with Russian aid from Georgia. The origins of the European conditions which gave rise to these situations will be discussed in the next chapter, since Wales is, of course, an example and it is in this context that the nature of this circumstance will be considered. But some brief examples can be outlined as evidence of its prevalence and the consequences that follow.

One of the most problematic of European examples is that of the Basque peoples. 'The Basques are concentrated in the four northern Spanish Provinces of Alava, Navarra, Guipuizoa and Viscaya.... They form an ethnically distinct group whose association with its present "homeland" goes back well beyond Roman times. Their geographically remote position has guarded them against assimilation by successive waves of conquerors. Equally, they have preserved an ancient language which is unrelated to any other European tongue' (Medhurst, 1982, 235). In their traditional way of life and their agricultural systems, too, they contrasted with Spain. The provinces never formed an independent unit and were generally under Castilian control but with special conditions of their own. In the late nineteenth century, with the growth of national movements generally in Europe, an independence movement arose and in 1894 the PNV (el Partido Nacionalista Vasco) was founded. Any signs of independence were ruthlessly put down, however, under the Spanish dictator, General Franco, and use of the language was outlawed. Moreover, at the same time as repressive actions had seen the emigration of many Basques, especially to the USA, the progressive industrialization of the coastal regions had led to the in-migration of non-Basques. Many regarded the PNV as reacting weakly and ineffectually to these changes and the threat they presented to Basque identity. So a more extreme organisation, ETA (Euskadi Ta Vaskatasuna) was founded in 1959 as an amalgamation of a series of discontented groups. ETA has undertaken a succession of terrorist actions against the Spanish government. In post-Franco Spain much more autonomy has been achieved and the three core provinces were made an autonomous community under the Statute of Autonomy of 1979. But despite a ceasefire a return to violence has recurred with complete independence as the basic demand of ETA. Given the admixture of populations as a result of recent movements, support for independence is not likely to be great enough to provide ETA with its desiderata. Here, is a second European example of the way in which an ethnic identity is related to territory and how violence follows.

One further example of a rather different nature can be outlined. What is now Belgium had been held by the Emperor Charles V as part of the United Provinces but the divergence of populations within that area was too great and under William of Orange the Netherlands broke away. What was left was held initially as the Spanish and then the Austrian Netherlands. Under Napoleon the provinces were again united but, as in the past, the antagonisms were too great and in 1831 the present state of Belgium was created. It has been called an arbitrary creation of history. Every geographic region of which it is composed has its counterpart outside the country. It had no focus of power, no core, no nuclear area. But, above all, it was founded across one of the major cultural divides of Europe, that between the Romance and the Germanic languages. Moreover, the contrasts were or became even greater. The Walloon, or French-speaking area became industrialised, was anti-clerical, and socialist. The Flemish area was mainly faithfully Catholic with a higher birth rate and a faster growing population. It was also agricultural, though later the centre of new industry.

At the time of foundation it was decreed that either language could be used but the antagonisms were so great that in 1921 an official language divide was created: to the south French is the official language, to the north Flemish. Owing to changes which had taken place the divide was redefined in 1962-3. Brussels was given a special bilingual status and there is a small German area in eastern Lorraine. A whole series of reforms took place during the 1970s and 1980s resulting in the 1992/3 St Michael's Agreement and a new constitution was introduced which is essentially federal. But during the whole of the post Second World War period the threat of the country breaking into two has existed as the interests of the two parts remain irreconcilable. Here language and culture again look to the exclusive control of territory.

Examples of these conflicts over territory occur universally across the world. The Kurds, whose language is banned in Turkey, have struggled long for any formal status. The Chinese have no intention of allowing Tibet its freedom and, again, the conflict between Uighurs and Han Chinese in Xinjiang is a recent example of territorial conflict. The Times newspaper reported on the problems of ethnic discontent in India. 'The ethnic Gurkhas (or Ghorkha) in this part of the state of West Bengal have relaunched a campaign to create their own state within India – to be called Ghorkhaland. In 2008 the newly formed Ghorkha Janmukkti Morcha (GMY) called a sporadic general strike....... "it's a question of identity", Bimal Gurung, the GJM leader, said.' (The Times, July 19, 2008, 42). The report adds that in 1986 a Ghurkha insurrection killed 1,200 people, although the problem was solved by the offer of limited autonomy.

The conflict between the Sinhalese and the Tamil peoples in Sri Lanka is one of the most widely reported and must have been responsible for more than a hundred thousand deaths. The conflict has followed virtually the same lines as in the other areas but developed into a full scale war. In May 2009 the Sri Lankan government claimed victory, largely due to the extensive logistical support given by the Chinese. The terrorist activities of the Tamil Tigers, the earliest employers of the suicide bomber, had the effect of limiting international support for the Tamils. Even so, Tamil expatriates in Parliament Square in London carry placards bearing the accusation 'genocide'. There is no need to rehearse once more the detail leading to the present situation for surely the point has been made: ethnic identities look for territorial expression and out of that some of the most bloody conflicts of recent years have emerged and the term 'ethnic cleansing' become a commonplace.

The third situation is possibly the one which has produced the greatest violence, where two incompatible cultural groups have become included under one political regime. The major progenitor of such situations has been the European struggle for African lands in the nineteenth and twentieth centuries when states were created with minimum consideration of tribal territories. Zimbabwe, although its troubles derive from other reasons nevertheless illustrates the condition. It was formed from territory granted to Cecil Rhodes's British South African Company by Queen Victoria in 1889. It was from that larger entity that Southern Rhodesia devolved in 1901. It included two major tribes, the Shona, part of the Bantu migrations into the area, and the Ndebele, who had moved north into what became Matabeleland. After the war of independence waged against the white minority, conflict ensued between the two groups and in 1983-4 President Mugabe under a Law and Order Maintenance Act sent his army into Matabeleland to ensure control. It is estimated that some 20,000 people were killed. But there have been far greater recent disasters. Rwanda and Sudan are the two that have dominated international news and have led to accusations of genocide.

Rwanda, one of the most terrible examples of inter-ethnic conflict, was a kingdom before European entry but after 1890 came under German domination, essentially part of German East Africa. The kingdom had been composed of two dominant groups, the Tutsi and the Hutu, who had lived apparently in accord. However, the Germans seemingly taken by the "Hamitic" background of the Tutsi, as against the Bantu Hutu, favoured them, thus creating antagonisms between the Tutsi, a group occupying all the positions of power, and a lower order made up of the Hutu. This situation continued under the Belgians, who were given a mandate after the First World War by the League of Nations and, indeed, after the Second World War when Rwanda became a UN Trust territory again administered by Belgium. Rwanda became an independent republic in 1962 and, given their numerical majority, the Hutu began to take over control. A number of attempts was made to undermine Hutu dominance from outside the country by Tutsi organised into what was called the Rwandan Patriotic Front (RPF) and there was a virtual civil war in 1990.

All these simmering antagonisms came to a head with the death in an air crash of the president of Rwanda, which rightly or wrongly was ascribed to Tutsi activity. The response was an outbreak of extreme violence led by the presidential guard and the creation of an organisation calling itself the Interahamwe. It is estimated that some 800,000 Tutsi and moderate Hutu were killed in what was an attempted genocide. Subsequently, the RPF did succeed in capturing Kigali and some two million Hutu fled the country. Later under the UN a multi-ethnic government was formed. But the subsequent history of that attempt at unity emphasises the stubborn and intractable nature of the situation and, indeed, its eventual descent into what has been called 'international war' (Prunier, 2009). This happening shocked the whole world. All the individual tragedies are lost in the conventional telling of the history. For the purpose of this book it is no more than the demonstration of how ethnic differences can result in the greatest of disasters. One hesitates to use such a catastrophe for academic purposes. Even so, it underlines the magnitude of the issues with which we are dealing.

The same can be said of Darfur. The Sudan was formerly under Egyptian control but the rise of the Mahdi detached it after the defeat of Anglo-Egyptian armies and the failure of General Gordon to secure reconciliation and his murder in 1885. The subsequent defeat of the Khalifa's army at Omdurman brought the Sudan back and in 1898 it came under joint British and Egyptian control. During the period of British oversight the north and the south were administered separately and it was not until the Juba Conference of 1947 that the decision to integrate the two parts was made. With characteristic ineptitude, the Foreign Office established the country across one of the major cultural divides in Africa, that between the Arabic and Muslim north and the black African and largely Christian south. Subsequently, with independence in 1956 continual conflict developed between the northern dominated government which regarded Sudan as an Arabic Islamist state, with all that implied in sharia law, and the under-represented and neglected south. Although the so-called Machakos Protocol in 2002 brought a degree of resolution, the south still experienced neglect which led in 2003 to unrest in the south-western area of Darfur.

The consequences have been horrific leading to some 400,000 deaths and some two and a half million displacements of individuals, as Arabic militias, the Janjaweed, have with government aid devastated the area. It seems generally agreed that the basis of the conflict is ethnic, even racial, rather than religious for the Moslems in the south have been treated no differently. Halima Bashir, whose book *Tears of the Desert* (2008) records in terrible detail the treatment of the people of Darfur, contends that the ruling elite of the Arab north regard the black African as no more than a savage. As a result of the activities of the Sudan Government the president of Sudan, Omar-al Bashir, has been charged by the International Criminal Court with genocide. One can only repeat the view at the end of the section on Rwanda: here are the bitter fruits of ethnic conflict over territory.

One other situation in relation to ethnicity and territory was noted earlier. These were the clashes which have arisen from immigration, since in-migrants tend to set up discrete areas within the lands of the host people. This engenders what is now usually referred to as multiculturalism and it will be dealt with at a later stage. Immigration can result not just in the establishment of 'Little Italies' or similar enclosures but in complete culture change. The movement into North America of white Anglo-Saxons completely displaced the native peoples, while the import of black slaves added another ethnic element. Likewise, the Aborigines of Australia were completely displaced. These brief statements refer so easily to the complete destruction of peoples, of ethnic groups - essentially genocide.

Although the attempt made at the definition of culture and ethnicity in Chapter 2 is a proper and necessary introduction to the consideration of Welsh identity, as indeed is the introduction of the notion of territoriality in this, it might well be asked if the exemplifications which have been presented are of strict relevance. They are because, firstly, the Welsh example which we intend to discuss is not a minor issue related to Wales alone. It is indeed representative of one of the most significant problems facing the contemporary world and the Welsh case must be seen in that context and, indeed, as an example of it. Secondly, the disastrous consequences of ethnic conflict need to be revealed, the true extent in slaughter and misery shown. That slaughter and misery occurred in Wales between some nine and six hundred years ago and it is against such a background as set out here that Welsh identity must be reviewed.

Chapter 4

Wales and the elements of ethnic identity

Before we deal with the substantive matter in this chapter it is necessary to undertake a brief methodological digression. There are two contrasted ways of approaching the complex field of identity. The first of these is to begin at the present day and, making no assumptions whatsoever, attempt to build up a cultural whole from its components, those which were discussed in Chapter 2. It can be summarised as 'starting with objects and people and tracing connections, not assuming collectivities in advance' (O'Neill, 2009, 150). It is a method which at least in some ways rather than being 'modern' echoes very much earlier attempts to define culture regions by a method called 'polythetic'. In this all the possible components, the objects and the people, or presumably their characteristics, are seen as giving different distributions. Where an area of maximum overlap can be identified to allow an area of sufficient homogeneity this can be established as a meaningful culture region - in our terms an ethnic identity. It was the method favoured by the doyen of culture region identification, the anthropologist A. L. Kroeber.

As Marvin Harris wrote, 'he approached the construction of cultural areas by means of increasingly elaborate statistical manipulation of disjointed trait-element lists of as many as six thousand items (Harris, 1968, 339). Harris added that no one has ever taken up his suggestion to measure intensity and climax by counting fragmented trait lists. A very limited illustration of this type of work can be seen in Chapter 6, 'Language Regions', in the book '*Spreading the Word*' by Aitchison and Carter (2004). There, just six, not six thousand, variables are used in a cluster analysis, a statistical procedure which derives groupings or clusters, of wards in this case, which demonstrate a degree of homogeneity. It is, of course, directed to internal differences within Wales, not to considering differences between Wales and the rest of the United Kingdom, but it is a useful demonstration of the type of approach. A much larger and more sophisticated example can be found in the Welsh Index of Multiple Deprivation.

The second method, in total contrast, 'assumes the collectivity' from the outset and proceeds to an analysis of how it came about, how it has been sustained and how it survives at the present. It is at this last stage that the notion of the validity of the collectivity comes under consideration. It will be manifest that the first method, which possibly seems preferable on logical grounds, is nevertheless extremely difficult to undertake on the scale necessary. Accordingly, the second approach will be adopted here.

Although the heading of this chapter refers to Wales, it is essential to begin on a much wider scale into which the condition of the country can be fitted. Certainly, to pursue the chapter title in its complex entirety would be to write the history of Wales. John Davies's magisterial *History of Wales* could well be interpreted as an extended discussion of the 'identity' of the country, as indeed could many national histories. For present purposes a much more general approach will be undertaken, and one which has resonance with the material treated in the last chapter.

A starting point is 'the decline and fall of the Roman Empire'. In spite of the immense complexity of those events, a predominant process can be abstracted. A variety of so-called barbarian peoples, especially those of Germanic origin, moved across the Roman frontier to occupy territories which had been part of the Roman imperium. It is possible to identify broad groupings, such as the Ostrogoths, Visigoths, Alemans and Franks, as well as the Anglo Saxons. Within these there was a multiplicity of tribes under their own chiefs so that post-Roman western Europe was divided into a kaleidoscope of territories. In this process two broad linguistic divides were created. The first was that between languages derived from Latin, where the Roman tradition was strong enough to absorb the incomers, and those derived from German, the Germanic language which replaced earlier tongues. The second was that between both those language groups and the Celtic languages that had once been widespread throughout Europe.

The interpretation of the locations of these divides is necessarily difficult and controversial. The latter, which is of concern in this study, has been usually interpreted as simply a process of the concentration of Celtic speakers into the western fringes under the pressure exerted by Anglo Saxon invaders, summarised in southern Britain by the creation of the dyke or boundary earthwork named after Offa, King of Mercia, one of those tribal groups which emerged in the process of conquest. Revisionist work has questioned the simplicity of this interpretation and has given greater play to the absorption of the Romano-British populations into the Saxon kingdoms. Even so, the general narrative can stand, with the isolation of the Celtic population in what is now Wales being brought about by their defeat at the battles of Chester (c616) and Dyrham (577) and the consequent naming of those confined peoples as "Welsh". The term has usually been interpreted as one of disdain, akin to the Greeks calling outsiders "barbarians". John Davies argues, however, that 'it would appear that "Welsh" meant not so much foreigners as people who had been Romanised, for other versions of the word may be found along the borders of the Empire, as in the Walloons of Belgium' (Davies, J. 1993, 71). 'The Welsh had also adopted a name for themselves, 'Cymry', which highlighted their awareness of themselves as "compatriots".... By the mid-seventh century at the latest, the Britons of Wales...had begun to describe themselves as Cymry, people of the same region or "bro". It was a most serviceable term. It could be applied to land and people alike' (Davies R.R. 1987, 19). It is worth adding in relation to the definition of the criteria of ethnic identity discussed in the last chapter that it was during these events of the incursions of the Anglo-Saxons that one of the great myths of Celtic identity was created in the role of the Romano-British leader Arthur who was supposed one day to return to restore the British to their rightful place.

Within the fragmented parts of the former Roman Empire the processes at work were largely the same. The more powerful tribal leaders succeeded in taking over their neighbours, gradually building larger entities which were to become the states of modern Europe. Clearly, the progress to statehood varied. It was most rapid and complete where there was a core with marked advantages. France is a manifest example. 'Certainly the force of Frankish warriors that Clovis used after about AD 480 to bring about a unified Gallic kingdom from the Garonne to the Channel was created by the unification of at least six separate war bands (Heather, 2005, 452). The eventual merging of the Saxon kingdoms into a unit called England is a parallel example.

States emerged in other ways. Charles V became heir to the Burgundian Netherlands and held the area that eventually became known as the Spanish Netherlands under seventeen different titles – Duke of Brabant, of Gelderland, of Limburg and of Luxembourg; Count of Artois, of Flanders, of Hainault, of Holland, of Namur, of Zealand and of Zutphen; Marquis of Antwerp; Lord of Friesland, of Groningen with its dependent districts of Mechlin, of Overyssel and of Utrecht. 'The seventeen states each had a separate constitution and differed considerably in social and political character but they were united to form a single autonomous unit over which Charles placed a regent. Moreover, he declared them to be a single and indivisible inheritance (Admiralty Handbook, Belgium, 1945, 93). Thus, the eventual state of the Netherlands was created by the association by a dominant ruler of a series of separate pieces, even if its complete realisation did not occur until the Congress of Vienna in 1815.

Likewise, the Iberian peninsular consisted of a series of separate territories, only one of which, Estramadura, had no political identity. The merging of these pieces only slowly proceeded and was finally sealed by the marriage of Phillip and Isabella, which created the Kingdom of the Spains, (note the plural). That unity was reinforced by what was virtually the creation of a new capital in Madrid. That doyen of historians, H. A. L. Fisher, sums the matter up admirably. 'The maritime state of Aragon, whose sailors and merchants were known in every port of the Mediterranean, had been united with the Kingdom of Castile by the marriage of Ferdinand and Isabella in 1469. A political union, founded on a marriage, cannot be expected to change the psychology of differing peoples. The inhabitants of Catalonia, the richest and most important part of the kingdom of Aragon, have never been assimilated with the Castilians, from whom they are divided by speech and all those profound differences which distinguish landsmen from seafarers, merchants from farmers, nobles from bourgeois, and a community stationed on a great world thoroughfare from one mainly living in secluded pride on a high inland plateau' (Fisher, 1941, 480-1). One of the old kingdoms was not encompassed and Portugal remained independent.

Somewhat controversially this process has been termed 'ethnogenesis' (Pohl, W in Little, L.K. and Rosenwein, B.H., 1998). Chris Wickham writes of the post Roman period, 'identities did change. Fewer and fewer people in the West called themselves Romani; the others found new ethnic markers: Goths, Lombards, Bavarians, Alemans, Franks, different varieties of Angles and Saxons.'(Wickham, 2009, 100). Perhaps the crux is that these tribal groups seldom metamorphosed into distinct ethnic territories but rather there followed the unification of territories by leaders who became 'kings' and created territories, which over time, and around a core, achieved elements of ethnic distinction and effectively created the 'nations' of Europe.

Academics instinctively dislike comparisons made over space and time, but even so there are comparisons with contemporary Africa. There is a discontinuity in that continent between tribal groups and the emergent political entities, many the arbitrary creations of the former colonial powers. As we saw in the last chapter, Zimbabwe is essentially the old Southern Rhodesia, a colonially manufactured territory, given a somewhat romantic name derived from a culture which was probably at it peak in the ninth century. Also in Chapter 3 we noted the conflict between two main peoples, the Shona and the Ndebele and that Mugabe's assumption of power was associated with widespread murder of the Ndebele. The integration of these peoples into a unity which means that they can call themselves Zimbabweans with a real cultural meaning is in reality a process of ethnogenesis. This is the problem that faces much of Africa, the translation of older tribal associations into newer meaningful territorial units on which perhaps new ethnic identities can be built.

This discussion has now moved into consideration of the nation and the nation state, on which the literature is as voluminous and as complex as that on ethnicity. Put at its simplest 'the nation' can be aligned with ethnic identity, as another expression of the unity brought about by the elements of culture which have been discussed in Chapter 2. In contrast the state, or the nation state, is a political entity, representing the ability to act independently within the system of states. The Welsh might constitute a nation but they do not form a nation state. The nation state nominally indicates a condition where the nation, the ethnic group, corresponds with the state, the political entity. There are very many problems which modify that simplistic notion, many of them related to scale. Even so, for this discussion the definitions offered can be used. There are, however, two reservations. The first is that in the ideal situation the unity of the people reinforces the strength of the state and the strength of the state reinforces the ethnic identity of the people. The second is that such an ideal situation rarely if ever occurs, for most states by the manner of their formation, which has been considered, inevitably include irredentist elements. These elements might be retained by force majeur, or by a realisation of mutual advantage. This is the second condition suggested in Chapter 3.

It is time to turn to consider how Wales fits into these convoluted notions. It would seem that the tribal territories which had pre-existed Roman conquest, and had survived as petty princedoms, would eventually be consolidated by a dominant ruler into one kingdom to the west of Offa's Dyke, just as the varied 'kingdoms' to the east were to become a unified Kingdom of England, and, indeed, the clan group and petty kingdoms of Scotland would be united into the Kingdom of Scotland. But although there were clear attempts made by Welsh 'princes' to achieve that unification it was never successfully accomplished. In many ways Wales was the opposite of what happened on the continent and, indeed, in England. There was no doubt about a clear ethnic identity but that identity lacked a unified political power and authority to build it into an independent, self-confident entity.

There is no intention here of tracing the extremely complicated history of those attempts to bring about unification, which was first outlined by Sir John Lloyd (1939) and subsequently clarified by a number of historians, most outstandingly by the late R. Rees Davies. Wales, he wrote 'was a country of many kings, many dynasties, many kingdoms' (Davies. R. R. 1987, 14). That these never gave rise to the single nation state, which would have sealed the question of identity, can be ascribed to one major social or legal constraint and three basic elements of geography.

The socio-legal problem was the Welsh custom of partible inheritance, or gavelkind. By that the estate of a deceased was divided among the surviving male heirs, in contrast with the English system where the eldest male inherited all. The result in Wales was a constant division and re-division of estates which militated against the building up of extensive lands under the control of a single leader. It also led to conflict among the surviving children. Rather than the process noted earlier of the amassing of lands to constitute larger territories, in Wales the opposite occurred, a continual breaking back into smaller extents.

The three geographical problems were all related to the physical nature of Wales. It is a country dominated by a central mountain core with a limited periphery. Moreover, to the east that periphery is open to infiltration along the major valley ways that penetrate the core. The rivers Dee, Severn and Wye and their tributaries give relatively easy access to the heart of the country. Unlike Scotland where the extensive Southern Uplands provide a buffer to the country's core, Wales has no such defence in depth and is open to invasion from the east. The second geographical element was the very limited extent of rich agricultural land. There was no reservoir of productive land, a rich core upon which a strong base could be developed. In brief, there was no equivalent to a Paris Basin, a London Basin or even a central valley as in Scotland on which a unified country could emerge. The third geographical limitation is closely related to the second. The relatively rich areas that did exist were small in extent and scattered in distribution, so that a range of competing centres developed rather than a single dominant one that could take control of the whole territory. It is highly significant that this lack of wealth and the subsequent limitation of trade meant that no urban tradition developed generating a city about which a unity could be forged. The towns which did develop were small and insignificant. There was no equivalent of London, Paris or, to make a more realistic comparison with a Celtic country, Edinburgh. At the first census of 1801 the largest town in Wales was Merthyr Tydfil, a new creation of the iron and coal industries owing nothing to past tradition, with but 7,705 people; Cardiff's population was 2,457 and that of the largest of the old regional centres, Carmarthen, was 5,548; that of Edinburgh was some 83,000. This situation will be discussed later in Chapter 11. In summary, Wales was a poor, fragmented country, unable to unite about any clear nucleus and open to incursion from the east. Rather than the different pieces of which it was composed becoming gathered into a single entity, a 'nation', it itself became one of the pieces assembled by a stronger neighbour into a 'united kingdom'.

As already indicated there is no intention in this discussion of following the complex processes of first the Anglo-Saxon incursions and then the Anglo-Norman invasions, the latter, of course, of much more significance in the matter of Welsh identity. Nor is there any purpose in tracing the ephemeral attempts by Welsh princes to establish hegemony over the whole country. The most important of these was that of Owain Glyn Dŵr but it too faded away, although leaving a legacy of an icon to be associated with identity and independence. The crucial markers are the Statute of Rhuddlan of 1284, when the conquest of Wales by Edward I can be regarded as completed, and the so-called Act of Union of 1536 passed under Henry VIII. It is significant, however, that during that long interval of two hundred and fifty years between the two enactments the identity of the Welsh was clearly recognised, even if only in the context of penalisation.

Thus, after the revolt of Glyn Dŵr a series of penal statutes was passed. For example, in 1400-01, 'It is accorded and ordained that from henceforth no Welshman be received to purchase land nor tenements within England, nor within the boroughs nor English towns upon pain to forfeit the said purchases'. And again, 'It is ordained and established that no Welshman be made Justice Chamberlain Chancellor Treasurer Sheriff Steward Constable or Castle Receiver Escheator Coroner nor

Chief Forester nor any other Office nor Keeper of the Records nor Lieutenant in any of the said Offices in no part of Wales'. And even to the extreme that, 'It is ordained and established that no Englishman married to any Welsh woman...or that in time to come marrieth himself to any Welsh woman be put in any office in Wales or the Marches of Wales'. However harsh and discriminatory these enactments were, they at least explicitly recognised the separate identity of the Welsh people. Such was not the case of the Act of Union of 1536.

That Act is properly entitled 'An Act for Laws and Justice to be Ministered in Wales In Like Form As It Is In This Realm'. Its purpose was stated bluntly. ...'by the authority' of the King it is 'ordained enacted and established that his said country or dominion of Wales shall stand and continue for ever from henceforth incorporated united and annexed to and with his realm of England'. The contingent conditions were unremitting. 'And also by cause these people of the same dominion have and do daily use a speech nothing like nor consonant to the natural tongue used within this Realm some rude and ignorant people have made distinction and diversity between the King's subjects of this Realm and his subjects of the said dominion and Principality whereby great discord and variance debate division murmur and sedition hath grown between his said subjects, his highness therefore of a singular love and favour he beareth towards his subjects of his said dominion of Wales minding and intending to reduce them to the perfect order notice knowledge of the laws of this realm and utterly to extirpate all and singular the sinister customs and usages differing'. The language, too, was to be eliminated... 'And also from henceforth no person or persons that use Welsh speech or language shall have or enjoy any manner office or fees within this Realm of England and Wales or other King's dominions upon pain of forfeiting the same office or fees unless he or they use and exercise the speech or language of English'. This was not an outright ban on the use of Welsh but effectively limited the domains in which it could be used with the clear assumption of a gradual decay and ultimate disappearance.

These enactments were manifestly directed at the total elimination not only of the Welsh laws that embodied so much of the Welsh way of life but also of all those customs and traditions which were distinctively Welsh, that is to destroy the culture and ethnic identity of the Welsh. To jump forward in time, it has become a cliché to quote the entry from the 1880 edition of the Encyclopaedia Britannica, 'Wales see England'.

It has aroused anger and scorn presumably because it was wrong and mistaken. But, in fact, it should arouse anger and scorn because it was manifestly true and correct since after the Act of Union Wales ceased to exist. It is interesting to observe that when at the 2001 Census a question was put as to ethnic identity the possible answer 'Welsh' was excluded, replicating with surprising acumen the position taken by the Encyclopaedia Britannica. In brief, the whole intent of the Act was to eliminate the Welsh as a separate people: to repeat the words of the Act, 'to extirpate all and singular the sinister customs and usages differing'. If we refer back to Chapter 2, 'the usages and customs differing' represent no more than a definition of culture, of the bases of ethnic identity. Wales was to become at best a province of England. From being a territory it became a territory within a territory. The question immediately arises as to how in fact the Welsh identity survived.

Chapter 5
The survival of the identity: after the Act

There were two crucial phases in the survival of Welsh identity. The first was the period following the Act of Union and the second the major upheaval caused by the Industrial Revolution. Glanmor Williams argued that the substantial changes introduced by the Act of Union were, first, the fixation of the territorial boundary. We have noted current conflict over territory. That conflict, and it had been associated with warfare and bloodshed, came to an end in 1536. Even so, the association of Monmouthshire with the Oxford judicial circuit meant that the county's link with Wales was ambiguous and the nomenclature 'Wales and Monmouthshire' lived on until recent times. *The Encyclopaedia of Wales* notes that even in the 1960s the Ordnance Survey classed Monmouthshire as an English county. That ambiguity certainly spills over into identity and there are some people in the marches of the Vale of Gwent who would gladly see the county restored to England. The other changes noted by Glanmor Williams were the provision of unity of jurisdiction and administration together with a coherence of government. Also, Welsh people acquired equality with English subjects under the Crown.

The critical issue of these changes was that they drove a wedge between the peasantry and the gentry. For the latter the Act opened up a wide range of new opportunities both within Wales in the new administrative and judicial system, and without Wales in Parliament and at the royal court, the latter in essence a diaspora, a term Glanmor Williams uses in summary. All this activity, as the Act demanded, was transacted in English so that language became the preferred medium of the gentry and an assimilation into an English identity followed. 'Many of the earlier historical bases of the difference between Welsh and English had therefore been eroded to the point of extinction as far the gentry were concerned'. This 'weakened beyond repair the connection between the gentry and the native literary culture. By the latter half of the seventeenth century, the old bardic order, the group which more than any other had given shape, expression and continuity to the former sense of Welsh identity, had become defunct' (G.Williams, 1993, 461).

There is here a further point of some significance. The eighteenth century is known as the age of enlightenment, the time which saw the widespread influence of scholars such as Descartes, Leibnitz and Newton. Not only natural science greatly developed but in all the professions issues were scrutinised free from the trammels of religious orthodoxy. All these ideas permeated down through the educated gentry and down the urban hierarchy, a diffusion based on social class and the English language. There were exceptions of course, but there was nothing in Wales to compare with the Scottish Enlightenment, with the work of David Hume, Adam Smith or James Hutton, which though in the English language, affirmed Scottish identity. In a Wales bereft of other markers the use of English by the educated seemed to confirm that Welsh was a barbaric language best forgotten as the merger with England progressed and identity was lost.

Set apart from the gentry, the Welsh peasantry continued with their old ways and with their old customs, those so well described by Trefor Owen in his '*Welsh Folk Customs*' (Owen, 1959). But, even at the heart of custom, change and assimilation was active. Henry VIII's religious policies had created a Church of England where the language of the new Bible and the Prayer Book was English. Isolation has always been the best defence of the integrity of identity and to a large extent that still operated in a Wales remote from the centres of government and power. But the dominant process was toward a total undermining of Welsh identity and of assimilation into English. There was one hope of a reversal of that trend in the revolt of Owain Glyn Dŵr at the beginning of the fifteenth century. In the famous Pennal letter of 1406 Glyn Dŵr virtually set out a programme of re-establishing the basic institutions of Welsh governance. There was also the proposal for two universities in the north and south as well as an independent Welsh church. All that disappeared with his defeat and as Rees Davies concludes, 'The failure of the revolt meant that the prospect of unitary native rule and political independence had gone for good. If the Welsh were to survive as a people, they would henceforth have to cultivate and sustain their identity, as in the past, by other means' (Davies, R.R. 1987, 465).

From this condition of survival a feature of the greatest significance emerges revolving around the 'other means'. For the Welsh everything that traditionally defined identity had been eliminated. The contrast with Scotland where Scottish laws and institutions remained is illuminating. Above all there was a Scottish monarchy and court and a Scottish education system, with St Andrews, the oldest university, founded in 1411 and Edinburgh in 1768. In consequence Scottish identity did not have any necessary relationship with the old Scottish language, Gaelic. Rather Lallans, a form of northern English, was the dominant form of speech. Identity did not depend on language, distinctive as that was but on a whole range of indigenous cultural and institutional features. In Wales in contrast there were no longer distinctive laws or institutions, no university education system, as the first college at Aberystwyth did not open its doors until 1872, the product of very different influences. There was no centre of power. The consequence was that there was but one thing, and one only, to affirm and sustain Welsh identity and that was the language. This intimate tie between language and identity was, therefore, to become a predominant factor but one with the most problematic of consequences. When in the future other sustainers of Welsh identity were to arise not based on language there was created an antagonism which has been at the heart of all the contemporary controversies relating to Welsh identity.

Yet another problem derived from this early period. The major incursions into Wales had taken place during the Norman conquest when effective occupation and settlement were limited to those lowland areas richest in agricultural potential and capable of sustaining the manorial system. These marcher lands created a cultural contrast between those parts of Wales where the Welsh language continued and those where it was displaced by English. This division of Wales into two, sometimes called an inner and an outer Wales or Y Gymru Gymraeg and Y Gymru Ddi-Gymraeg, created a condition that consistently impinged on notions of unity and of common identity. Here, there are parallels with the other Celtic countries. In Scotland the Highlands and Islands were often at odds with the central lowland core but in Ireland the division was more drastic and gave rise in the post World War One settlement to the creation of a separate largely Protestant Northern Ireland and largely Roman Catholic Irish Republic. Whereas language was an element of difference in both Scotland and Ireland it never played the crucial and central role which it did in Wales.

Against this background of the problem which faced Welsh identity after the Act of Union, why in fact was the cultural assimilation of Wales into England never achieved? In the introduction to this book it was contended that two of the critical elements of ethnic identity were language and religion. In the period following the union with England the language, a cornerstone of identity, was clearly under threat and it was through religion, the other basis of identity that the situation was saved. With the Henrician settlement it became evident to the church hierarchy that for the mass of the population neither Latin nor English were tenable as languages of common use and salvation could only come through the vernacular. And that, surely, was one of the bases of the Protestant reformation. A groundswell of opinion arose among the Welsh bishops for the critical bases of the new Church to be made into Welsh. As one petition put it, the Bible should be available 'in the vulgar Welsh tongue that the prince of darkness might not altogether possess the Principality of Wales'.

There is a clear implication in the quotation. The translation of the Bible and Prayer Book has nothing to do with the status of the language but everything to do with the saving of souls. An upshot of Henry's religious policy was, therefore, in part to undermine the effectiveness of the measures in the Acts of Union and of Great Sessions. This manifested itself in 1563 in the 'Act for the Translation of the Bible into Welsh' and with it also the Book of Common Prayer. This was accomplished in 1588 with the publication of Bishop Morgan's translation – Y Beibl Cyssegr-lân. A revision to match the English Authorised Version, was published in 1620 and a portable form in 1630. *The Encyclopaedia of Wales* records four editions in the seventeenth century and twelve in the eighteenth. Glanmor Williams wrote: 'The year in which English independence was preserved by the defeat of the Armada was also the year in which the linguistic and cultural integrity of Wales was saved by Morgan's Bible.' (Williams, 1993. 322). Norman Tebbit once proposed a cricket test to reveal those who were truly English by their support of England rather than another country. In similar vein it is possible to identity Welshness by asking about the significance of the year 1588. The true-born Welsh will answer the publication of the Welsh Bible, the true-born English the defeat of the Armada.

There followed from the late seventeenth century two lines of development that were to preserve Welsh identity. The first was in direct line from the translation of the Bible and led in the following century to one of the greatest influences in the preservation and extension of the Welsh language, the circulating schools initiated by Griffith Jones, the Vicar of Llanddowror. His motive was also the saving of souls, not the safeguarding of the language. His scheme was based on itinerant teachers who stayed at a location for about three months to teach reading so that the Bible was made widely accessible. David Williams epitomised his work thus: 'He helped to make the Welsh a literate nation' (D.Williams, 1950, 47). But there was much more than that, as the Methodist movement which followed, based on the Bible and its accessibility, revitalised the Welsh people and through the preaching of ministers and an outflowing of hymns aroused them into a new self awareness. There was also another aspect. The general population knew very little of the history of Wales, indeed that history was virtually unwritten. The Bible, and especially the Old Testament, provided them with the history of a small, primarily pastoral people struggling for their very existence, creating their identity. Here was a clear parallel; if there was no history of Wales, that of Israel could be taken as a surrogate and through it an identity forged.

At this point it is perhaps useful to refer to the notion of imagined communities as set out by Benedict Anderson in a book with that title (Anderson, 2006). Anderson, in spite of the title, was mainly concerned with nations and nationalism. Nevertheless, what he proposed is relevant to ethnic communities. His central idea was that even in small communities actual interaction between all the members is impossible. He, therefore, suggested that rather than actual communities there were imagined communities, 'in the minds of each lives the image of their communion' (Anderson, 2006, 6). Thus, through the affinity with the Israel of the Old Testament, along with the myths of their own origin, the Welsh people re-established an identity. Moreover, Anderson argued that the image, lacking person to person communication, is based on written material, hence the importance of all those influences which had created a literate peasantry. Through the Methodist revival and the other branches of Nonconformity the Welsh people became alive to their own particularity. Moreover, a special link was established between the language and Nonconformity; religion and language became interlinked and a new domain was added to Welsh identity. Although its apotheosis was to take form only in the next century, the grounds for the stereotypical Welsh person were laid, chapel going, hymn-singing, 'Bible black' and politically radical. And a stereotype is a sure indicator of an identity.

Other changes that took place in the eighteenth century were also to have a major impact upon the language and upon Welshness. This was the period of the late Renaissance leading into the age of enlightenment. It was characterised by the abandonment of the old myths of Gildas and Geoffrey of Monmouth, and 'the rise of a more serious, self-conscious Welshness based on books, eisteddfodau and literary or debating societies' (Morgan, 1981, 13). If the old bardic tradition was attenuated the writers in prose brought a new scholarship to bear on things Welsh. Edward Lhuyd introduced a new scientific basis not only to his work in botany, but also to his studies of the Celtic languages. On a somewhat different level, Theophilus Evans' '*Drych y Prifoesoedd*' provided an inspiring view of the Welsh past. It 'exercised an extraordinary influence on the ordinary Welshman's view of his nation's past. By opening the eyes of Welsh readers to the glories of the past, it had a tonic effect on the nation's morale (Jenkins, 1993, 247-8). All these developments are perhaps best represented not by what took place in Wales but in initiatives in London. Under the stimulus of the Morris brothers of Anglesey, The Honourable Society of Cymmrodorion was founded in 1751, followed by the Gwyneddigion in 1770, a gathering for the men of the north. In brief, through all these varied activities a new realisation of the identity of the Welsh was being established with a new confidence in its significance. In that context, the language remained the one clear element of difference and of identity.

The two trends were of course interlinked, although there was always an antagonism between the secular scholars and the spiritual Christians. Together, however, they had rescued Welshness from the nadir of the period following the Act of Union. The attempt by the English crown to eliminate the idea of a Welsh people had been firmly rejected. Yet, even within this era a new threat arose from the development of industry and the complete transformation of the economy.

Chapter 6
The long Nineteenth Century

The threat to language and identity in the nineteenth century came directly from the vast changes both in population numbers and distribution which were brought about by the process of industrialisation. The population of Wales increased from 587,245 at the 1801 census to 2,012,876 at the 1901 census. Glamorgan's population of 70,879 in 1801 had become 859,931 by 1901, an elevenfold increase. In contrast, by 1871 all the rural counties were experiencing actual population loss; the process of rural depopulation which was to be characteristic for a hundred years had set in. There is an immediate response to assume that the loss of population from the Welsh-speaking rural counties was aggravated by the immigration of English speakers to the developing industrial areas, bringing with it a consequence for the solidarity of Welshness. But much of the movement, certainly in the early part of the century, was internal and it can be argued that for the first time large settlements which were at least in good part Welsh speaking were the result. Hence Gwyn Alf Williams's assertion that Merthyr Tydfil was the first Welsh town (G. A. Williams, 1966). At the 1851 census the major industrialised communities in Merthyr returned some ninety per cent as Welsh-born. The figure for Dowlais, for example, was 91.9 per cent and for Pentrebach 92.4 (Carter and Wheatley, 1982).

If, therefore, there was a weakening of Welsh self-belief it is necessary to look elsewhere. Victorian society perceived two fundamental limitations of the Welsh language and, by extension, to the conviction of being Welsh. The first was the virtual exclusion of Welsh from the new and developing domain of technology, and indeed from the whole spheres of science and business. The bulk of the entrepreneurs in the new industries came from across the border. Even many of the lesser tradesmen were in-migrants, In Merthyr Tydfil at the 1851 census the enumeration district of East Market Field, which was at the centre of the town's shopping core, returned some 24.4 per cent of household heads as English born.

From the above condition the second limitation followed. The nineteenth century saw not only the development of a wide range of industrial skills but also, and in many ways more significantly, the immense growth of clerical work. There was created a class system in which each stratum attempted to distance itself from the level below. Into this social system the language was integrated, as was the notion of Welshness. To speak English, preferably with the accent of genteel English society, became the ideal to be pursued. Welsh became a language which children did not need to acquire; indeed they were far better off without it since it carried the implication of low social class. Here the lack of a Welsh aristocracy was crucial. In modern jargon there were no role models to follow since those who did dominate the higher reaches of the economy and of society were anglicised. Immediately after the Second World War there was a widespread belief that Wales was a classless society. This was, of course, nonsense and it soon disappeared from the literature. But even for it to arise meant that there was some element of reality and that arose from the fact that there were no Welsh aristocrats for there had never been a Welsh court in modern times. Unlike Scotland, Wales never had an indigenous royal circle. There is a strange concatenation between the Commissioners who reported on the state of education in Wales in 1847 and those commentators who at the present refer to the Welsh as troglodytes or in the words of Sunday Times columnist, A. A. Gill, as, 'loquacious dissemblers, immoral liars, stunted, bigoted, dark, ugly, pugnacious little trolls'. They both are essentially unable to comprehend a society lacking the class range which characterised England, a society which had no aristocratic overburden.

There were repercussions for the Welsh. As Gwyneth Tyson Roberts concludes in her book on the Report, 'Many Welsh people...reacted against the report: many others, however, accepted at least at some level, its message about themselves, their community and their language as it filtered down to them via comment, quotation and general summary. For them it constituted a devastating "cultural bomb"... which blasted them into submission by telling them with all the power of its authority that the distinctive features which gave themselves, their community and their country a separate identity...were irredeemably inferior, backward, and barbaric, and should be discarded as objects of shame and guilt' (Roberts, 1998, 238). Many are the tales, perhaps apocryphal, of Welsh people anxiously attempting to lose their accents in order to pass as English, essentially to sacrifice identity, for in British society for a long time that was the way forward; and given the external view of Welsh identity presented in the Blue Books that was not surprising. Kenneth O. Morgan writes 'The idea of Wales in later Victorian Britain was a singularly ill-defined one. To one local bishop in 1886 Wales was no more than a geographical expression' while many viewed it 'as a semi-civilised, picturesque survival'. And again, 'even as late as 1919, ignorance of "the unspeakable Celt" was fashionable, almost a conventional, wisdom' (Morgan, 1981, 3). It is no wonder that at least some ambitious Welsh people were willing to downplay their identity.

There was another domain in which the language and concomitant identity were to lose relevance, even if only to a degree. The radical nature of Welsh Nonconformity had been embodied in support for the Liberal Party; Nonconformity and Liberalism were inextricably associated and the Welsh language was the matrix of that association. By the end of the nineteenth century and the beginning of the twentieth much of radical opinion was turning to Socialism. If Lloyd George was the apotheosis of Welshness at least to a degree, the election of Keir Hardie to the parliamentary seat of Merthyr Tydfil in 1900 was the sign of change. But the new Socialism saw itself as international and cosmopolitan, and in consequence, removed from the introspective Welsh tradition. 'From 1911 onwards Socialism and the new miners' union were becoming the new religion. The language of Socialism was English... To abandon Welsh became not only a valuational but also a symbolic rejection and affirmation (Jones, 1992, 78). Here, too, the consequences are still present, and react today on the nature of Welshness. The old, traditional socialists are still dominated by a rejection of what is conceived as parochial and limited in comparison with the international character of Socialism and want no truck with things specifically and uniquely Welsh. Hence arose the somewhat anomalous but deep antipathy between Plaid Cymru and some elements of the Labour Party, although both parties claim to be Socialist in principle.

It would seem from the above discussion that the major trends of the nineteenth century, the massive population changes and the radical restructuring of employment patterns, would be inimical to the affirmation of Welsh identity. But those trends gave to things Welsh a new strength. The population of Wales in 1801 was 587,245, in 1901 it was 2,012,876. For long the conventional wisdom was that this increase, presumably caused by immigration from across the border, undermined the language and the separateness of Wales. Such was not the case. The bulk of the population growth was due to natural increase, the excess of births over deaths, and immigration from England was not significant until the end of the century. There certainly was a major redistribution of population but this served to give a new power to the feeling of difference. This was first proposed by Brinley Thomas (1987) and has since become widely accepted. He argued that the language was in fact saved by becoming an urban language spoken by the population en masse rather than a rural survival, in which environment it which might well have decayed. The end of the nineteenth century was in fact the period when the highest *numbers* of Welsh speakers were recorded; the maximum was 977,366 reached in 1911, although a higher proportion was returned in 1901, effectively half the population, a total of 929,824. In what must be the definitive history of the period K. O. Morgan entitles the chapter dealing with this period, 'The National Revival' (Morgan, 1981). It is attested by a wide range of evidence. The chapels of the new industrial areas supported an increasing number of journals. Hywel Teifi Edwards records that in 1896 there were 32 periodicals and 25 newspapers published in Welsh (Edwards, 1987, 122). Morgan writes, 'that during the 1880s dramatic transformations swept through the land which added up to a kind of renaissance', which 'expressed itself at the most popular grass roots level. The Welsh language in some ways proved more vigorous than ever in the years after 1880. It had a new status and protection. In 1885 a group of cultured patriots...founded a Society for the Utilization of the Welsh Language' (Morgan, 1981, 94).

There was another context in which a particularity of Wales was developing, one indeed which perhaps was paramount from a popular viewpoint. This was, of course, music, and especially choral music. It has been admirably traced by Rhidian Griffiths (Morgannwg, 2007, 6) where he sets the growth of musical culture post 1860 as a background to the composition of *Hen Wlad Fy Nhadau*. It was a period, he points out, when the Eisteddfod was becoming dominated by music and during which 'chapel music began to be tamed from its post-eighteenth-century excesses to a somewhat rigid formalism that was the basis of four-part congregational singing, for which Wales acquired a legendary reputation' (Griffiths, 2007, 10). Here was *Cymru Gwlad y Gân*, the land of song, which marked the recognition of a distinctive feature of a culture, an element of ethnic identity couched popularly in the widespread if erroneous belief that all Welsh people can sing. This was the period when the James brothers composed *Hen Wlad Fy Nhadau*, which by prescription became a national anthem. To an ancient flag was added a modern anthem as the symbols of a people.

In terms of Welsh identity there were other significant developments that were not directly associated with the language. The radicalism which was inherent in Nonconformity was allied to an awareness of the spread of national revivals across Europe to produce the kind of renaissance adduced by Morgan. In political terms it is most clearly associated with Cymru Fydd, a society initially formed in London in 1886 but soon extended throughout Wales. As the *Encyclopaedia of Wales* records, 'initially it was in the main a cultural organisation' but 'repeated efforts were made to transform it into a national Welsh political organisation'. It stood for land and education reform, for the disestablishment in Wales of the Church of England and, indeed, for home rule. But, in brief, the surge for the recognition of the independence of Wales, in a general rather than a political sense, can best be identified in the establishment of Welsh institutions over a wide range of affairs.

In education, the University College of Wales opened at Aberystwyth in 1872, the forerunner of a University of Wales given its charter in 1893. Notably, the college at Aberystwyth was not endowed by royal or aristocratic hands but according to its proud boast 'founded on the pennies of the poor'. In the cultural context, a National Museum of Wales and a National Library of Wales were both given charters in 1907. In the sporting field, the Football Association of Wales was founded at Wrexham in 1877, The Welsh Rugby Union at Neath in 1881, locations not without their own cultural implications in the divisions between north and south. In religion, although the disestablishment of the Church faltered over the allocation of its funds, the Welsh Church Act was passed in 1914. (Because of the War its implementation was delayed until 1920 but Welsh Nonconformity had been appeased by the Sunday Closing Act of 1881.) To this list can be added Urdd Gobaith Cymru, founded in 1922 in order to advance the language and the sense of Welshness among the young. The above constitutes little more than a selected list but it clearly illustrates the strongly flowing tide towards creation of a Welsh identity, the affirmation of separateness, at the end of the nineteenth and the beginning of the twentieth centuries.

Reservations have to be made. Cymru Fydd virtually fell apart at its conference in 1896. One statement only by a delegate needs to be recorded. 'There are from Swansea to Newport, thousands of Englishmen, as true Liberals as yourselves, who will never submit to the domination of Welsh ideas' (*Encyclopaedia of Wales*, 2008, 186). That last sentence emphasises the substantial divisions that broke out across Wales and which were to be its curse for generations to come. In lighter tones the contrast between the association football of the north and the rugby of the south has been referred to above. More substantially, as K. O. Morgan writes over the collapse of Cymru Fydd, 'the gulf between north and mid-Wales on the one hand and mercantile, industrial south Wales on the other seemed alarming and gaping,' (Morgan,1981, 118). There have always been stresses and strains between north and south, as between Cymry Cymraeg and Cymry Di-Gymraeg, and these have acted effectively against the confident assumption of common identity.

In spite of these reservations it would seem that at the beginning of the twentieth century Wales was emerging with a language spoken by some half of the population and well backed by a range of journals and publications. Allied to that was a clear tide of feeling and opinion moving toward and reinforcing the feeling of separate identity. However, the next fifty years were to see a massive reversal of both these aspects of life in Wales. The causes are effectively summarised by Brinley Thomas; '...a major cause of the decline of the Welsh language was the collapse of the Welsh economy after the First World War. Because of the dazzling heights reached just before the First World War, the subsequent fall was all the more disastrous. The class war in the coalfields intensified and the clarion call was Marxist not Methodist. What the potato famine did to the Irish economy, the Great Depression did to the Welsh economy. In the twentieth century, economic and demographic contraction, the decline of Nonconformity, severe unemployment and emigration...have been a curse to the language' (Thomas, 1987, 437). Although Thomas wrote with specific reference to the language, the sentiment can be directly transferred to the whole gamut of belief in distinction and identity. Poverty and insecurity dominated life and undermined self-belief. There followed a stream of out-migration. Gwyn Thomas relates his apocryphal story of climbing the Rhondda valley side to the cemetery above Trealaw to find a grave stone marked, 'Not dead but gone to Slough'. A PEP (Planned Economic Policy) report said that the situation was such that the whole town of Merthyr Tydfil should be abandoned. There is no point here in tracing the often related story of industrial decay, only that its impact upon the self confidence of the Welsh needs to be stressed.

It would be a mistake to concentrate, however, on the industrial areas only. Rural depopulation which had begun in the second half of the nineteenth century continued unabated, reaching a peak in the period after the Second World War. Massive changes in the nature of agriculture, especially extensive mechanisation, led to a savage drop in employment, farm amalgamations and rural decline. A downward spiral in economic and social well being followed as the necessary population to support basic amenities diminished. The young and active emigrated, leaving an elderly population, with the result that natural decrease accompanied out-migration, the epitome of demographic decay. Rural depopulation became the theme of nearly every study of rural Wales in the years before and after the Second World War.

By the mid century, therefore, the bright dawn of the late nineteenth century had been transformed into a darkening day of overcast gloom. The condition is summarised by the condition of the language. The 49.9 per cent of Welsh-speakers of 1901 had by 1951 declined to 28.9 per cent. That bright confidence, which is at the heart of self belief, had been lost. Much of the heart of identity was, if not lost, at least compromised but as always there was a resilience.

Chapter 7

A reclamation of identity

The general narrative of the history of Welsh identity which we have followed has largely been characterised by attenuation and diminution. At the same time there was a constant trend towards the retention of that identity, a reclamation, and it is to that aspect we now turn, largely by a consideration of the way in which immigrant groups into Wales have been assimilated and melded into a Welsh way of life. This reference to immigrant groups immediately calls into attention the fashionable modern notion of multiculturalism. That surely is nothing new. Medieval Wales with a possible Saxon remnant, with Norman French and indigenous Welsh populations, was presumably an archetype of the multicultural. But for a consideration of the way in which Welsh identity has survived I will turn to the towns of Wales since as an academic my specialty was urban geography (Carter, 1965) and it makes an appropriate context.

Continuity of settlement, if not of urban status, from Roman times on is becoming as apparent in Wales as it is in England. But the relevant beginnings of urbanism in Wales can be ascribed to the Anglo-Norman conquest and the planting of towns as an effective and central part of the process of occupation. The purpose of town building was not solely military control and the elimination of the threat from the west to the English kingdom by the construction of defensible strong points. Economic control and cultural transformation were explicit aims, inherent to pacification and occupation. It was similar to many contemporary and later patterns of colonial take-over. If we view this in relation to methods of urban social area analysis, it would be expected that all the items or indicants of social variation would vary, together giving a single basis both to social variation and its spatial expression. That is, the conventional variants of social rank or status, ethnicity and migratory status would all be associated in single construct. There would be effective segregation on all linked bases. If status be defined as determined by the holding of land, as is usually suggested for pre-capitalist cities, this was probably the case in the early years of the Anglo-Norman towns. Let me quote from the re-enactment of the penal statutes after the Glyn Dŵr uprising at the beginning of the fifteenth century.

'It is accorded and assented that from henceforth no Welshman be received to purchase land nor tenements within England nor within the boroughs nor English towns of Wales upon pain to forfeit the said purchases.....Nor that no Welshman shall be accepted Burgess nor to have any other liberty with the Realm

69

nor within the boroughs and towns aforesaid.'
(AD 1400-1 2 Henry 4 c20. Bowen 1908 pp. 33-4)

Like most such systems of ethnic discrimination it was accompanied by other prohibitions on participation in administrative and economic life, for effective control was to be retained in the hands of the dominant group.

> 'That all grants of franchises, market fairs and other Liberties to buy or to sell... within the towns of North Wales made to any Welshman before this time shall be voided and of no value.'
> AD 1446-7 25 Henry 6 (Bowen, 1908, 45)

As we have seen earlier, these prohibitions even extended to marriage in that no Englishman married to a Welsh woman could hold any office 'in Wales or the marches of Wales'. All these enactments established the basis not simply of ethnic segregation but of an institutionalised segregation. *Mutatis mutandis* these statutes constitute the components of a Group Areas Act of apartheid South Africa, and the enforcement of separate development. They also recognise a multicultural condition.

The question arises as to the extent to which the ends explicit in the legislation were enforced and made effective. Unfortunately, the limited data which are available at such an early date remove the possibility of any formal social area analysis. There are, however, two lines of evidence which can be followed. The first is the ethnic character of those who held land in the towns, as recorded in burgess registers and taxation lists, and of those who participated in urban government. The second source is the physical character of the towns themselves.

Evidence for the first of these two lines can be derived from the volume *'The Boroughs of Medieval Wales'* edited by R.A. Griffiths where the relative Welshness of the towns was specifically posed as a question for the contributors. Caernarfon in the heart of Welsh Wales is an appropriate example with which to begin. K Williams-Jones in his chapter on the town writes, 'There can be no doubt that in 1298...it was entirely peopled by non-Welshmen.. Apart from the translations from other boroughs, burgesses continued to be recruited from outside the province for a century and a half after its foundation. Lists of burgesses at various times make that abundantly clear. So, too, do the names of those who served in the office of bailiff of the town. Not until the first year of Henry VIII's reign do we come across a

Welsh name and even thereafter persons with Welsh names only rarely served as bailiffs before 1536 (Williams-Jones, 1978, 93). Here is a clear association of status and ethnicity and a clear separation of the major elements composing the town. But during the long period between the Statute of Rhuddlan (1284) and the Act of Union a slow transformation took place, increasing in pace towards the later date with land within the borough being acquired by Welshmen. As late as 1532, however, Williams-Jones notes how the burgesses of Caernarfon turned on fourteen of their own co-burgesses for demising fifteen properties in the town 'to certain strangers namely foreigners, who 'had no liberty within the town'. The 'foreigners' so contemptuously referred to were all described as 'yeomen': worse of all they bore Welsh names (Williams-Jones, 1978, 101).

To contrast with Caernarfon it is appropriate to consider another town, Brecon, located in the marches of Wales. Professor Rees Davies wrote: 'The racial composition of the burgesses is eloquent to the process of cultural assimilation. The alien character of the original burgess population of Brecon does not, of course, admit to doubt.... The first extant burgess list that appended to the 1411 charter shows the continuing preponderance of English personal names: only six out of a total of eighty six bear unmistakably Welsh names. But changes were taking place so that by 1443 a quarter of the burgesses has Welsh names' (Davies, R.R. 1978, 67). Again, by the tax assessments of 1543 only some thirty out of the 192 taxpayers may be classified in any way as having English names. There was, therefore considerable variation in the process of change. Griffiths concludes that Aberystwyth 'was almost entirely Welsh in character' by the end of the Middle Ages. Indeed, as early as 1307 the first survey of the town indicated that some 43 per cent of the burgages [tenures] were occupied by Welshmen. But as Williams-Jones observes, to the Welsh gentry securing a foothold within the town meant acceptance on equal terms with Englishmen and Griffiths concludes that although the Welsh element in Aberystwyth grew stronger the burgesses continued to be disliked by Cardiganshire people because of their privileges 'for some of them were rural landowners of substance' (Griffiths, 1978, 39).

The second line of evidence is the physical nature of the towns. Williams-Jones discussing the conflict at Caernarfon between the resident burgesses and the Welsh writes that 'the suburbs, the very area from which a Welsh community had been moved in 1283 and which had been destroyed by Glyn Dŵr ... was once again occupied by

Welsh people in the early Tudor age. This is where most of the sixty or more 'fforen inhabitaunts' mentioned in a petition of 1518 were found' (Williams-Jones, 1978, 96-7). Rees Davies, discussing the population of the town of Brecon, observes that 'were we able to include ... the very considerable extra-mural population' estimates of the Welshness of the town even in 1411 would be very different (Davies, R.R. 1978, 67). Here is a clear contrast between an intra-mural English population and a suburban Welsh one. This is made apparent by noting the names of the major town houses, the *plasau*, of Caernarfon. All were located within the town walls and their names are ample testimony to their origin – Plas Puleston, Plas Spicer , Plas Bowman. In contrast to them was the mass of cottages which had accumulated outside the town walls. At Aberystwyth the equivalent suburban area to the south of the river Rheidol was called 'Trefechan', a name which with but a little degree of flexibility can be translated as 'township' with all the implications which that name carries.

The conclusions which can be reached from this brief survey are that an initial contrast between population groups and their intra urban locations based on linkage of status, ethnicity and migrant origin characterised the towns of Wales at the time of their foundation. Over the quarter of millennium between 1284 and 1536 the ethnic dimension and its linked migrant origin dimension in their most obvious manifestations slowly diminished, so that by the time of the Act of Union status was the dominant control of a contrast between characteristically pre-industrial high status centres and low status marginal suburbs. But before we accept such a neat summation it is well to realise that for Welshmen to become part of the urban patriciate, if that is not too high sounding a term to use in relation to these small towns, carried with it a price. Even at the time of the Act of Union no one who did not speak English could hold public office and upward mobility brought with it strong anglicising pressures, even if the advent of a freer market and economic growth generated a Welsh speaking but non landowning urban population. In this diminution of the ethnic element it is tempting to make an outrageous comparison with a study of the USA in the 1970s. In 1978 W. J. Wilson, a black sociologist at the University of Chicago published a book entitled '*The Declining Significance of Race*'. His main theme was that racial discrimination, and the disadvantage arising from it, was no longer significant in the USA and that socio-economic status was the paramount dimension of contrast. True, there was a permanent disadvantage underclass, but that it was predominantly black was the consequence of particular historical circumstances.

There were, as one might expect, quite violent refutations but, if it is accepted, there is a comparison with what occurred in Wales after the Norman incursions. Slowly, Welsh people began to move into the towns which no longer were the exclusive domain of the conquering immigrants, and status, rather than ethnicity, became the basis of distinction. In short, the Welsh began to take back their own land, even assimilating the incomers so that a Welsh identity was not lost. Partly as a consequence, the towns have always been more anglicised than the neighbouring countryside but that is inevitable in what are meeting places. To put this into more modern terminology Wales immediately after the Norman incursion was multicultural, English and Welsh lived segmented lives in contrasted and mutually exclusive areas. Over time that segmentation was eroded and a degree of integration followed and status became a separated basis of locational differences. The Welsh might also at this later stage have formed a historically derived underclass but the distinctions were basically those of status rather than ethnicity. Multiculturalism had been at least partly mitigated.

The second phase of urban genesis in Wales (Carter, 1952), is the industrial period beginning in about 1750. Development during that phase, too, was mainly, if never wholly, externally derived, for town growth was consequent upon the work of entrepreneurs and the investment of capital from outside Wales. Two examples can be taken. The first is Merthyr Tydfil, which was the largest settlement in Wales throughout most of the nineteenth century. The second is the greatly contrasted town of Aberystwyth, a small market town which had developed as a seaside resort from the 1790s.

The general structure of Merthyr Tydfil at the middle of the nineteenth century was the epitome of a multi-nuclear town, the major nuclei being the sub-towns, for surely one cannot call them suburbs, grown about ironworks at Dowlais, Cyfarthfa, Penydarren and Pentrebach. Of these, Dowlais was nearest to being an independent settlement, while Pentrebach to the south was much looser and more diffuse in structure. At the point of convergence of roads from these nuclei a central business district had grown extending northward along the High Street from the pre-industrial village which had collected about the church of St Tydfil. In 1851, at a time when the structure was still forming, there were open interstitial areas between the constituent parts. An analysis of data from the 1851 census (Carter and Wheatley, 1982) reveals that there were three distinct groups in the town. First there was the high status, English-born population engaged in professional and managerial occupations. It is possible to add, by inference, that it was predominantly Anglican in religion. Certainly, a new church, ironically called St Davids, had been built in the middle of the High Street in 1847. It was recorded in the 1851 Census of Religion as 'an additional church, 'for English service, while under the parish church of St Tydfil it was noted that 'the majority of the English congregation had moved to St Davids on its consecration. (Jones, 1976, 170).

The second group was made up of the skilled and semi-skilled workers in the iron industry. It was essentially Welsh in character being made up of migrants from rural Wales. By inference, it was overwhelmingly Nonconformist. In 1851 the Upper Merthyr Tydfil sub-district returned the two Anglican churches, one Roman Catholic and twenty-one Nonconformist chapels. Thirdly, there was a group made up of those lowest in the social order, unskilled labourers by occupation and in which the Irish formed a clear section. Here, is a replication, *mutatis mutandis* of the condition in the towns of the first genetic phase. There is no institutional discrimination based on penal statutes but the end result is similar. The town was possessed by the iron masters and the emergent immigrant bourgeoisie, small as it was in Merthyr, and those possessors were characteristically, though not exclusively, English.

The spatial expression of this social structure was strangely similar to that of the earlier period. The high status group was predominantly central in its location, mainly occupying premises at first floor level along High Street. It was paradoxically a classic pre-industrial pattern since suburbanisation was to come much later. The only discordant element was the iron masters in their mansions overlooking the ironworks. The lowest status, especially the Irish, were essentially inner city, being concentrated in two very distinctive areas with appalling physical conditions, to the north and south of the central business district. The skilled workers, and the Welsh, dominated the peripheral industrial nuclei, among which Dowlais stood out most clearly. At this point it is necessary to enter a caveat. The concept of these three distinct groups is something of a caricature. There were, for example, many of the lowest status residents in the central area, even if they were in courts and alleys, for manual labour and servants had to be at hand. But even so the broad conclusions stand. Here is a multicultural Merthyr, English, Welsh and Irish living in segmented sections of the town.

The nineteenth century, like the post-mediaeval period, is marked by the struggle of the people to possess their own cities. It, too, was marked by violence, the most well-known episode being the Merthyr riot of 1831 (Williams, 1978). But change was more rapid, for the Anglo-Normans were settlers whereas the iron-masters were prepared to move out after fortunes had been made. The apotheosis of change was possibly marked by the Parliamentary elections of 1868, following the second Reform Act of 1867. It was confidentially expected that Henry Austin Bruce, later Baron Aberdare, would be returned. He had represented Merthyr since 1852 but he came bottom of the poll, which was topped by Henry Richard. Ieuan Gwynedd Jones writes, 'the return of Henry Richard...was rightly regarded as a great victory for the Nonconformists of the borough...but...factors other than Nonconformity were present in the election... The concentration of contemporaries on the factor of Nonconformity to the exclusion of those arising out of industrial grievances should not obscure the true significance when soon after he described himself as emphatically the advocate of the cause of the working class and of Welsh Nonconformity' (Jones 1981, 213). There were three elements in Richard's cause, Welshness, for he conducted most of his meetings in Welsh, Nonconformity and working class interests. Here again is the Welsh working people taking over the town and making it in their image. As that happened, the segmentation that had characterised the town slowly disappeared so that by the end of the century it was status which was the discriminator not ethnic identity: Welsh, English and Irish and even Jewish - for Merthyr had the first Welsh synagogue - had merged.

The small resort town of Aberystwyth in a totally contrasted situation displays the same patterns, faintly if not clearly. In 1851 of the heads of household born in Aberystwyth 15.7 per cent were in social classes 1 and 2 (using the allocations suggested by Armstrong) and there were 12.4 per cent in 1871. Of those born in England 32.4 per cent and 33.5 per cent were in those two classes at the census dates. Examination of distribution suggests that the English born were dispersed throughout the town but they were certainly not in evidence in the poorest parts and were clearly linked to the newest and best town housing. They certainly lived away from the south western quadrant of the old walled town, which by inference was the most Welsh area as evidenced by the returns from the 1891 census which first recorded language. That census analysed by Robert Smith (1999) gives a fascinating picture of a town struggling to keep its Welsh roots against an increasing presence of monoglot English.

This latter element had been brought in by the railway and the resort function. Smith records that there were 41 railway workers recorded in the census mainly employed by the Cambrian Railway Company, which made a direct effort to employ English speakers and to ensure that English was the language of the railway. Over half of the town's railway workers were monoglot English, including the station master. While the majority of the hoteliers and lodging house keepers were local the impact of visitors meant that the majority had become bilingual and there were strong forces leading to the loss of the Welsh language. Smith observes that the town displayed a very complex pattern and it was so since it was in the middle of the fight to preserve its identity under the impact of commercial development. Even at that late date ethnicity was a factor in distribution. Smith notes that there was only some quarter of the population who were monoglot Welsh and that they lived in the poorer areas such as Trefechan and Penparcau. As in Merthyr it was eroded over time, as status became dominant with suburban expansion, and by the early twentieth century the contrast in the town was between the newer suburbs and the crowded courts of the centre. The town was in essence, however, a Welsh town. It is worth observing that by 2001 only 39.6 per cent of the population of Penparcau spoke Welsh, although it retained its character as one of relatively low status.

These two examinations of towns in the nineteenth century confirm a general process. At times of flux caused by immigration, populations remain separated and segregated. That can be called multiculturalism. Over time the differences of culture and origin are modified. There is interaction between indigenous and in-migrant population but even so, given the numerical dominance of the local, the basic ethnic identity is usually though not always maintained. What has been demonstrated is that the Welsh have effectively reclaimed their own towns even though as meeting places they are the points of maximum exposure to external influences. The bringing back of the towns into the framework of Welsh identity was a major factor in the language's preservation. It is no surprise that today Welsh is predominantly an urban language.

The third example is very different in that the threat has been predominantly to rural areas and in particular those where the Welsh language was at its strongest. The basis of the threat lay in a feature common to the western world. In the USA it was called 'counter-urbanisation', but perhaps the Australian term, 'rural retreating', is more self explanatory. In the latter decades of the twentieth century urban living and urbanisation which had dominated in the previous century, lost its attraction. Congestion, pollution and burgeoning crime turned the middling classes especially against city living. In addition, there was a less material influence. City life was associated with intense competition, the so-called 'rat race'. Many found that way of living less and less attractive in spite of all the facilities which the city offered. Moreover, there was a hangover from the hippy culture of the late 60s which had been based on rejection of the competitive materialism of the metropoles. The result was twofold. First there was the direct out-migration of people seeking a new way of life, especially from the English conurbations, to rural areas and small towns. Property in the cities was far more expensive than in the rural area so that those moving brought an ability to afford housing greatly in excess of that of the local populations. The same goal could be achieved by buying second homes where an escape to the country was provided but a foothold kept in the city. Both these were to have a marked impact upon Wales.

Population migration in Britain, the Welsh case of which we are concerned with here, is a major area of study in its own right (Champion, 1992; Stillwell, Rees and Boden, 1992) and the impact upon Welsh speech but one aspect of a much broader field of investigation. In particular, counter-urbanisation has been one of the most potent processes to have introduced non-Welsh speakers into Wales. This is evident even to those whose concern is with more general issues. Stillwell writes, 'During the 1970s and 1980s in-migration has led to a reversal of the long term population decline in many parts of rural Wales. A clear tendency towards an increase in net in-migration in the 30-44, 45-54, and over 55 age groups is also apparent from the mid-80s' (Stillwelll, 1991, 30). He notes that 'by 1988-89, the focus of high net in-migration had shifted to Wales and the west of England' (Stillwell, 1991, 17) and he adds, 'The in-migration of people into rural Wales, many of them from outside the Principality, and the impact of such in-migrants on the destination communities is seen by many as a great threat to Welsh culture. The rural "revival" is widely regarded as having the potential to destroy the linguistic and cultural traditions of these rural areas' (Stillwell, 1991, 30). It must be added that this is not solely a Welsh problem. Allen and Mooney write of 'a particular vocabulary associated with counter-urbanisation in which terms such as "locals", "incomers" and "settlers" have become common parlance'. They continue: 'groups such as "Scottish Watch" and "Settler Watch" have projected images of harmonious rural life which is being disrupted and destroyed by incoming populations... The use of the term "White

Settler", in particular, conveys feelings of colonisation where local culture is interpreted as being usurped by a more dominant "English" culture' (Allen and Mooney, 1998, 281-2). Such difficulties are not unknown in England (Capstick, 1987).

There are three main sources on which the analysis of this migration process can be based. The first is direct ground survey. Certainly, the best recent example in Wales, although rural deprivation and not language was the prime concern, is a Lampeter-based study (Cloke, Goodwin and Milbourne, 1995, 1998). They write, 'Our respondents in Wales strongly associate community change with cultural change due to the influx of 'foreigners'... Moreover, there is no doubt that many of our Welsh-speaking respondents, particularly within the area of Y Fro Gymraeg, clearly identify the influx of the foreign with an invasion of 'the English'. Here, we can view 'Englishness' as a 'significant other'... which is perceived by local Welsh-speaking residents as threatening the existence of their everyday language and culture' (Cloke, Gooodwin and Milbourne, 1998,141). The problem with such surveys is that they are costly both in time and money, are inevitably selective by being based on samples and are prone to all the difficulties associated with questionnaire methodology. Even so, all such studies have stressed the significant influence of in-migration upon language. The second basis for migration analysis lies in the National Health Service central register. Evidence of movement is derived from the registration of people with medical practitioners. The data are collected on Family Practitioner Committee areas (family health service authorities), which generally conform to counties. The material is valuable in that it provides a continuous monitor as against the decennial census. But the areas are large and, of course, there is no language element recorded.

The third source is the census, which does provide a mass of information. However, there are major drawbacks. The basis of the published data is change of address in the year before the census so that it is only a snapshot of one year, not a review of the decade. Change of address is not a particularly satisfactory way of interpreting migration. A move 'next door' in the same street must be interpreted as migration; perhaps logically and properly it is, but it has limited significance in the general interpretation of migration. Moreover, until 1991 no link with language was included. But in the 1991 census, Table 4 in the Welsh language volume gives not only the number of migrants but the number of Welsh speakers among them. For the first time, therefore, some assessment could be made of the relation between migration and language on a general basis. Even so, there are limitations. Thus, a central concern of any analysis must be to establish the net effect of migration on the numbers of Welsh speakers.

Table 7.1 attempts to do this for Gwynedd. But as can be seen a problem immediately arises. There were 3,583 persons who were living elsewhere in Great Britain who had been residents of Gwynedd one year before the census. But since they were living outside Wales where the question as to the ability to speak Welsh was not asked, there is no way of identifying the impact on language.

Table 7.1
Migration of Welsh speakers into and out of Gwynedd 1991

County	Migrants out	Migrants in
Clwyd	314	272
Dyfed	85	81
Gwent	10	4
Mid Glamorgan	18	15
Powys	50	45
South Glamorgan	90	58
West Glamorgan	14	12
Rest of Great Britain	*	840

See Assumptions below.

Assumption 1:
Numbers for Rest of Britain equate to the percentage of Welsh speakers in Gwynedd: 61% of 3,583= 2,186

Assumption 2:
Numbers for Rest of Britain equate to the percentage of Welsh speakers migrating to other Welsh counties: 39.2% of 3,583 = 1,405

Total out-migrants under assumption 1: 2,767
Total out-migrants under assumption 2: 1,986

Total in-migrants: 1,327

In Table 7.1 two assumptions, imputations the census might call them, have been made. The first assumes that the proportion of Welsh-speaking out-migrants would be equal to the proportion of Welsh speakers in Gwynedd, that is 61 per cent. The second assumption assumes that the proportion moving to the rest of Great Britain would be the same as that moving to the other Welsh counties where data as to language is available, that is 39.2 per cent. These are two very different proportions and the conclusions clearly no more than tentative. All that can be said is that whichever figure is taken, there was still a net out-migration of Welsh speakers and hence a loss to the county. But on one assumption it was 1,440 and on the other 659. If, perhaps illegitimately, the single year is extrapolated to the decade, the differences at 14,400 and 6,596 are considerable.

There are further problems with the census data. They are only published on a county basis. Thus, for example, the joining of Ceredigion, Llanelli and South Pembrokeshire in the county of Dyfed considerably undermines the value of the returns, almost to the point of rendering them useless. Accordingly, additional data giving a district by county matrix was purchased from the Office for National Statistics. This is used in much of the discussion that follows but in assessing movement, and to avoid dominance of very local movement, migration from the county in which the district is located is ignored. This is undoubtedly a questionable procedure but the costs of a district by district matrix were prohibitive and unless the procedure suggested is followed minor local movement of little import for language would swamp the larger scale migration that is crucial to the language situation.

There is yet one more difficulty. The in-migrants were already in place when the census was taken so they have already influenced the linguistic situation. This presents some inconsistency when the pattern of migration is related to the characteristics of the in situ population.

The most sensible way to analyse the data is to concentrate on those areas where Welsh was widely spoken, that is the traditional Fro Gymraeg, the cores of dominant Welsh speech. Table 7.2 provides relevant data for the two northern cores, Ynys Môn and Arfon-Dwyfor, along with Meirionnydd which forms the third core, and Ceredigion together with Preseli.

Table 7.2
Migration data for Districts of Welsh-speaking Wales (Y Fro Gymraeg)

District	Per cent Welsh-speaking	Per cent Welsh born	Number of In-migrants	Per cent from outside Wales	Per cent in-migrants Welsh-speaking
Ynys Môn	62.0	67.7	1726	88.5	17.3
Arfon	74.6	76.6	1183	82.8	27.6
Dwyfor	75.4	71.5	640	87.2	28.4
Meirionnydd	65.4	64.3	1026	78.7	24.1
Ceredigion	59.1	64.2	2052	81.2	21.3
Preseli	24.4	71.8	2070	83.3	8.9

These districts indicate the problems which have characterised the heart of Welsh-speaking Wales over recent times. One flow of in-migrants dominates all others virtually to their exclusion. All, except Meirionnydd, where the difference is only marginal, return over 80 per cent of all in-migrants from outside Wales. No Welsh county contributed more than 10 per cent to the total flow. The highest proportions were essentially cross border movements, thus Clwyd contributed 7.6 per cent to Arfon, 7.4 per cent to Ynys Môn and 6.1 per cent to Dwyfor. In these northern cores the greatest absolute numbers were registered by Ynys Môn, a condition reflected in the lower percentage of Welsh speakers in the district, as well as the lower proportion born in Wales. An aspect missed because of the data selected is the process of suburbanisation spreading from Bangor across the Menai Straits. There were 3,681 in-migrants from Gwynedd into Ynys Môn but of those only 2,062 or 56 per cent spoke Welsh, well below the proportion recorded for the island. Indeed, only Dyfed, which accounted for only 27 in-migrants recorded a proportion of Welsh speakers above that of the district and that was only 63.0 per cent.

It would seem that the two districts which make up the second node in the north, Arfon and Dwyfor, have been somewhat more resilient, possibly because of a location more removed from the A55 and its impact. The basic pattern is similar to Ynys Môn, however, with a high degree of dominant migration from outside Wales. No Welsh county accounted for more than ten per cent. In Arfon, only Clwyd with 90 movers contributed more than five per cent at 7.6 per cent, but only 57.8 per cent were Welsh speakers, well below the district level. Dwyfor showed a similar pattern with 39 migrants (6.1 per cent), of whom only 48.7 per cent spoke Welsh. When local movement is considered, 3,031 from Gwynedd were recorded in Arfon, of whom 1,999 or 66 per cent spoke Welsh, while the figures for Dwyfor were 1,073 and 75.8 per cent. Inevitably, since these are the districts within Wales with the highest proportions of Welsh speakers, it is likely that a lower proportion of Welsh speaking in-migrants will be recorded but the overall flows show a quite significant anglicising process. If internal movement within Gwynedd is ignored, the overall external movement into the districts returned percentages of Welsh speakers at 17.3 per cent (Ynys Môn), 27.6 per cent (Arfon) and 28.4 per cent (Dwyfor). These are dramatically below the proportions of speakers within the districts and must inevitably have accounted for a decline in the 'Welshness' of these areas.

Meirionnydd demonstrates a pattern similar to that of Ynys Môn, with a dominant in-migration from outside Wales. Possibly as a result of its location and extensive borders with neighbouring counties, it shows some evidence of rather greater flows from Welsh sources with 85 or 8.3 per cent from Clwyd and 64 or 6.5 per cent from Powys. This is standard cross border movement but in each case the Welsh speaking proportions, at 52.9 and 50.7 per cent respectively, are both lower than the District's 65.4 per cent. When all movements are considered the percentage of Welsh speakers among these migrants was only 24.1 per cent.

Since of all the pre-1997 counties Gwynedd was the only one which bore some relation to a distinctive language area, it is worthwhile considering the data for the county as a whole. These are set out in Table 7.3. The conclusions drawn from the district data are reinforced. Some 80 per cent of the in-migrant flow came from outside Wales and only 16.6 per cent of the 5,060 spoke Welsh, compared with the county's figure of 58.8 per cent. As would be expected, the largest flow from within Wales came from neighbouring counties, especially Clwyd to the east with 824 or 13.1 per cent, but with only 272 or 33 per cent Welsh speakers among them, and Powys 99 with 45.5 Welsh speakers. Dyfed, to the south, provided 132 but the proportion of Welsh speakers was 61.4 per cent, higher than the proportion in Gwynedd itself. Only South Glamorgan out of the other counties provided an equally high percentage of Welsh speakers, though only a small number. The proportion among all in-migrants was a mere 21.1 per cent.

Table 7.3
In-migration to Gwynedd. 1990-1991

Source of migrants	Numbers of in-migrants	Percentage of Migrants	Numbers Welsh speaking	Percentage Welsh speaking
Clwyd	824	13.1	272	33.0
Dyfed	132	2.1	81	61.4
Gwent	15	0.2	4	26.7
Mid Glam.	33	0.5	15	45.5
Powys	99	1.6	45	45.5
South Glam.	95	1.5	58	61.1
West Glam.	34	0.5	12	35.3
Outside Wales	5060	80.4	840	16.6
Totals	6292	100	1327	21.1

Out-migration presents the problems already discussed. Table 7.4 displays the data that are available. The dominant outflow, some 3,853 or 72.2 per cent, was to destinations in the rest of the United Kingdom, but there are no data for the number of Welsh speakers. The main destination within Wales was Clwyd, again a neighbouring county.

Table 7.4

Out-migration from Gwynedd 1990-1991

Destination of outmigrants	Number of outmigrants	Percentage of outmigrants	Number Welsh speaking	Percentage Welsh speaking
Clwyd	963	18.1	314	32.0
Dyfed	161	3.0	85	52.8
Gwent	36	0.7	10	27.8
Mid Glam.	36	0.7	18	50.0
Powys	104	1.9	50	48.1
South Glam.	149	2.8	90	60.4
West Glam.	33	0.6	14	42.4
Rest of UK	3853	72.2	??	??
Totals	5335	100	??	??

It is especially worth noting the 149 who moved to South Glamorgan - 103 to Cardiff and 46 to the Vale of Glamorgan. This is some indication of the flow to the capital and its suburbs, a point to be taken up later.

These county data reveal the same crucial issue as did those for the districts. There is a two pronged problem for language maintenance. The first is a clear loss of Welsh-speakers through out-migration, a loss compounded by the predominance in the inflow of non Welsh-speakers from outside Wales.

The southern part of Y Fro Gymraeg, south of the Dyfi estuary, is made up of Ceredigion but it extends also into the northern part of Preseli Pembrokeshire. Unfortunately, the district boundary does not coincide with the Landsker but in spite of that the district is joined with Ceredigion in this analysis. From the data in Table 7.2 a clear parallel between Ceredigion and Meirionnydd is evident. It is possible that the somewhat lower proportion of Welsh speakers in Ceredigion at 59.1 per cent can be related to the higher total of in-migrants from outside Wales at 1,667 or 81.2 per cent of the total. But given the contrast in populations, 63,940 in Ceredigion as against 33,583 in Meirionnydd, the totals, like the proportions, are more in line. It is also significant that both districts lost population by excess of deaths over births, to the extent of -2.3 per cent in Ceredigion and -3.3 per cent in Meirionnydd over the decade. There is no way of knowing whether that loss had any effect on language, although all the evidence suggests that the elderly and, therefore, those likely to make up the deaths recorded, were more likely to be Welsh speakers. Even so, the situation in terms of natural processes made the impact of migration all the more pertinent. If the migration from outside Wales into Ceredigion for the one year of the census migration table is extrapolated to the decade of the population figures, a total of 16,670 would represent an increase on the 1981 population of the district of some 29.0 per cent.

This is undoubtedly a highly questionable procedure but it serves to indicate the very considerable impact that this migration process possibly had on the decrease of the proportion speaking Welsh in Ceredigion from 65.5 per cent in 1981 to 59.1 per cent in 1991. It also accounts for the relatively low proportion who were Welsh born, at 64.2 per cent, not even making up two thirds of the population. The percentage of Welsh speakers among all in-migrants was 21.3, only exceeded in the districts analysed to date by Ynys Môn at 17.3. Few comments can be added on Preseli for the reasons stated but the high number from outside Wales, together with the low proportion of Welsh-speakers, a mere 8.9 per cent, testify to the same processes at work.

The evidence which can be presented in relation to these districts that make up 'Welsh Wales' is obviously limited. Above all, the extent and nature of out-migration, in a language/identity context, cannot be set alongside that for in-migration, while the evidence relating to natural increases or decreases is likewise uncertain. Even so, the general conclusion is very evident and beyond challenge, that the heartland of the Welsh language was discernibly weakened by the movement into the area of non Welsh speaking populations. If the numbers of in-migrants from outside Wales in the districts are added together for the one year 1990-1991 some 7,262 moved into these parts of Wales. If the admittedly unacceptable procedure of extrapolating this figure for the decade is followed, the total for the decade is 72,620, a figure higher than that of the population of any of the districts. Only 14.8 per cent spoke Welsh. If the border area of Preseli is taken out, the 1981-1991 figure is 5,538, giving a decadal total of 55,380, out of which some 955, or only 17.2 per cent spoke Welsh. In summary, there can be no doubt immigration created a major problem inasmuch as incomers who spoke no Welsh were unlikely to immediately adopt a Welsh identity.

Another element of the escape from the conurbations can be seen in the growth in the number of second homes, many in areas where Welsh sentiment was strongest. The aristocracy had always been possessed of country estates and town houses but the affluent bourgeoisie began to ape that situation in the owning of second homes in rural areas. The numbers are not easy to establish, partly due to problems of definition. A bulletin of the Statistical Directorate of the Welsh Assembly Government attempted comparison of the various data sources (WAG Statistical Directorate, 2005). It notes that, 'the main differences between the data sources is that the 1991 census and 1988 Welsh Housing and Dwelling Survey suggest that there were over 25,000 second and holiday homes in Wales, while the council-tax returns give a figure of just under 17,000' (WAG Statistical Directorate, 2005, 5). For our purposes the 2001 census data can be used to give at least some idea of the problem. In the census the term household spaces is used and those with no residents were classified as either second residences or vacant household spaces. The latter were those recorded by the enumerators as absent, refusals or non-returns.

The two counties with the highest proportions of second homes (the term 'household' is used by the census) were Gwynedd at 7.8 per cent and Pembrokeshire with 6.1 per cent. The bulletin quoted above notes, however, that 'census statistics for second homes seem low, for instance in Gwynedd and Pembrokeshire where the corresponding figures for vacant dwellings are relatively high (WAG, Statistical Directorate, 2005, 8). Those latter figures are respectively 5.5 and 5.1 per cent but within the counties there are three areas where proportions are very much higher. The first is the coastal area of Pembrokeshire where The Havens, which includes Broadhaven, records 24.8 of household as second homes with a further 6.2 per cent as vacant. Solva records 21.1 per cent of households as second homes and Newport 24.1 per cent and a further 8.8 per cent as vacant, making a possible total of nearly a third (32.9 per cent). The second area is the hinterland of Dolgellau with the ward of Brithdir, Llanfachreth, Ganllwyd and Llanelltyd returning 17.1 per cent as second homes and Corris/Mawddwy with 20.1 per cent and a further 6.9 per cent as vacant. The third area is the south coast of the Llŷn peninsula. Llanengan returns as high as 28.3 per cent as second homes with 6.3 per cent vacant, while Aberdaron has 19.7 per cent and 5 per cent vacant. Other parts of Wales are similar in their coastal and rural environment. New Quay on the Ceredigion coast has 22.6 per cent of households as second homes and Gower has 13.8 per cent.

It is manifest that figures of these magnitudes must have a marked impact both by their occupation and by their ownership, mainly by English people. Such conditions must weaken the Welshness of these areas, a fact borne out by the lower proportions declaring themselves to be Welsh which were recorded in the Labour Force Survey (see Table 8,1 following). It was in response to this situation that some elements of violence occurred, paralleling that seen in earlier eras. The Free Wales Army was little more than a charade but Meibion Glyn Dŵr (Sons of Glyn Dŵr), significantly named, was responsible for setting fire to a number of unoccupied second homes starting in 1979 and peaking in the late 1980s.

It was a transitory response and the real fight back was on a much broader basis. This was more of a real regeneration, making a separate consideration necessary.

Chapter 8
Regeneration

As noted in chapter 6, after the Second World War there was a pattern of increasingly serious losses in the proportion of the population able to speak Welsh, reaching a nadir in the decade 1961-1971 when the percentage fell by 5.2 per cent and the actual number of Welsh speakers by 17.3 per cent. Subsequently, the trend although not reversed, has been considerably ameliorated. In the decade 1981-91 the percentage of the total population speaking Welsh fell by only 0.4 per cent and the actual number of Welsh-speakers by 1.4 per cent.

The changes, however, varied considerably across Wales. A band of the highest decreases surrounded the core Welsh-speaking areas of the rural north and west, virtually along the boundary between core and periphery. In the core itself there was a complex pattern of decreases and increases but with large extents still showing decline, partly demonstrating areas that have been subject to in-migration, and certainly marking out the internal fracture lines which during the second half of the century had broken up the once continuous extent of 'Welsh Wales' (Aitchison and Carter, 1994). In contrast, the highly anglicised and urban areas of the country returned quite distinctive increases; paradoxically they define what were virtually the traditional anglicised marcher territories.

The above outline states the situation very starkly but does pose crucial questions as well as presenting a basic paradox. The questions relate to the causes which lie behind the evidence of at least a partial transformation in the fortunes of the language, so that from a state where imminent demise was forecast it has reached one where regeneration is apparent. A recent survey by data firm Euromosaic records Welsh as scoring fairly well on a scale measure of minority languages and is noted as affording 'some optimism concerning language use' (Nelde, Strubell and Williams, 1996). The paradox, already noted, is that the greatest increases have been achieved in those areas where the language has traditionally been weakest. Some explanation of these changes is clearly needed. To some degree this has to be carried out by examining what the authors argue is the continually changing basis of language groups. 'Our starting point is to develop a conceptualisation of the changing nature of language groups. Rather than resorting to the static concepts of language maintenance and language shift, with their reification of language, we resort to a conception based on the reproduction, production and non-production of language groups. This has the advantage of relating these three processes to the more general processes of social and cultural reproduction' (Nelde, Strubell and Williams, 1996, 5).

Arising from these principles it is necessary to consider the way in which those processes of social and cultural reproduction, and consequent language reproduction, have been conditioned by fundamental economic changes on which they are, in turn, based. G.E. and K. Lang gave their book on Watergate the title '*The Battle for Public Opinion*'. It would not be inapt to summarise the process of language revival in Wales under the same heading, for it is control of that public opinion that has impacted upon the processes of reproduction. That struggle over opinion has to be set within a very distinctive socio-economic and political background, which was critical to its nurturing.

The political background can be succinctly described as post-modern. In the past neither of the major political parties in Britain have had a great regard for the Welsh language. To Conservatives it was no more than a rural patois; as has been pointed out earlier, to many in order to get on, to ascend the greasy pole, to obtain wealth and social influence, English was essential. Welsh was at best an irrelevance, at worst an actual hindrance. What Matthew Arnold had written in the second half of the nineteenth century was still believed at the end of the twentieth century. 'The Welsh language is the curse of Wales. Its prevalence, and the ignorance of the English language, have excluded and even now exclude the Welsh people from the civilisation of their English neighbours'; and 'the sooner the Welsh language disappears as an instrument of the practical, political, social life of Wales, the better... (Arnold, 1867). As contended earlier, Socialism's main concern was with internationalism, with brother workers and comrades in Britain and elsewhere. The formative pamphlet produced in 1912 by Noah Ablett of the South Wales Miners' Federation, *The Miners' Next Step*, was never translated into Welsh. The medium of communication in Socialism became English, and Welsh, with its associations with Liberalism and Nonconformity, a marginal relic of little consequence. Indeed, the attitude of some supporters of Labour was not very different from that of Arnold. It was against that socio-cultural background, and the location of socio-economic power in the hands of those who saw little relevance in it, that the decline of the language that marked much of the twentieth century took place.

The end of that century has witnessed a sea-change. The dogmatic certainties of both right and left have been relinquished as the one brought increasing social division and created a disaffected underclass, and the other, as witnessed in eastern Europe, brought economic atrophy and social decay. In consequence, there has been the substitution of a pragmatism in which the clash of ideologies, within which attitudes to the language were emplaced, has been minimised so that conflicts of principle become centred on specific, single issues rather than on grand designs. Into such a situation the so-called single issue fanatics were able to insert their concerns. Animal rights, pro-life anti-abortion, gun control, environmental matters such as anti-road building, have all dominated political action. One of these issues was the Welsh language, as advanced mainly by Cymdeithas Yr Iaith Gymraeg (the Welsh Language Society). Indeed, the society, founded in its present form in 1962, was one of the earliest of the single issue protagonists and has since become legitimised among a number of quite disparate activist groups. The peak of direct action was in the late 1960s when parallel anti-establishment movements were on the move across western Europe. In essence, language zealots appeared as part of a general stir rather than a set of isolated oddities as they had often been regarded in the past.

At the same time Wales was undergoing a major economic transformation, which can be epitomised by the single term, de-industrialisation. The old heavy industries, especially coal and iron and steel, were in process of decline or rationalisation. Employment patterns were radically changing and in place of the decaying smoke-stack industries new fields of work were expanding. These were in the service sector, bureaucracy and the media. Blackaby et alia wrote in a survey of the Welsh economy, 'as for the total distribution of employment in Wales, the largest employing sector is the service sector, where roughly seven out of every ten employees are employed....the overall picture...is one of a service-sector based economy... traditional heavy industry playing a small role in industrial employment (Blackaby et alia, 1995, 236). Employment in agriculture in Wales fell by 5.26 per cent between 1992 and 1995; in energy and water it fell by a massive 27.27 per cent. In contrast, employment in banking and finance rose by an equally impressive 19.72 per cent.

Whereas in the past the conflict between owner/manager and worker had neatly fitted the parties of the right and the left, a new bourgeoisie that was partly Welsh-speaking was being created. It was made up of the people who operated the social and health services, who ran the enlarged and increasingly complex system of government in Wales that followed the creation of the Welsh Office in 1964, and who contributed in a major way to the development of education from ysgol meithrin (nursery school) to university. The same changes were responsible, too, for the greatly enhanced status and scale of the mass media. Into the jobs thus created moved Welshmen and women, mainly educated in Wales and speaking Welsh, to create a new Welsh-speaking sector high in the social scale and with very different attitudes to the language from those that had been dominant at the beginning of the century. The two trends which have been examined above, political and economic, were certainly not divorced one from the other. The young student activists of language support have been transformed into the more mature operators of the system and the parents of the Welsh-speaking children. The changing nature of the economy has provided an opportunity for those committed to the language to secure positions of influence. The crucial aspect of those positions was the way in which the battle for public opinion could be manipulated. The field of that battle was and is the mass media. At this point, therefore, with the socio-economic background which has been set out in mind, it is appropriate to turn to examine the various relevant aspects which the Langs identify.

The first of these aspects of the battle for public opinion is the setting of the agenda. 'The agenda-setting hypothesis derives from the observation that the mass media, while perhaps not very effective in persuading people *what* to think, do seem to tell people what to think about' (Lang and Lang, 1983, 7). McCombs and Shaw describe the agenda-setting function in the same manner, that people learn from the mass media what the important issues are (McCombs and Shaw, 1972). Clearly, the formal way of measuring that function would be to determine the time devoted to language issues by the news and current affairs programmes of BBC Wales, Radio Cymru and ITV Wales. Such an analysis with necessary recourse to transcripts of broadcasts over a long period, a form of content analysis, is hardly feasible. But anecdotally it is possible to maintain that the language was made into an issue that was being put continually before the public. That the media are fully convinced that they control the agenda can be discerned in an advertisement in the Western Mail on Thursday, February 12, 1997, for an editor for the programme 'Wales Today', described as the 'BBC Wales flagship news programme'. The job description states bluntly, 'it sets the news agenda for Wales'. Newspapers followed and the language became a standby topic for discussion. The Welsh-speaking bourgeoisie, whose rise has already been traced, played a significant role in the decision-making echelons of the media and was consistently able to insert the language into the agenda of matters of public importance and to keep it there.

Alongside setting the agenda, there is another theoretical notion which is called the refraction principle. This suggests that against the background of the increasing mass of news and information which is generated, most people have neither the time nor the expertise to develop informed views; they are reliant on the media. But not only do the media select which matters to bring forward, those matters are inevitably presented in a specific way. Most social scientists would accept the idea that, however honest the intention, there is no such thing as objectivity. That is, the information stream is refracted through the mediation of editors and presenters. And in the case of the language those who were setting the agenda were also to some degree the presenters. Public opinion was, therefore, steered away from the attitude that had dominated with regard to the language over the nineteenth and early twentieth centuries where Welsh was perceived as a dying language best left to decay to one of committed support or at least tacit acceptance.

The third theoretical determinant of public opinion can be called the significance of critical events (Lang and Lang, 1983, 9). This maintains that opinion can be tangibly directed by specific events which become causes célèbres and sway judgments. In relation to the language two can be selected. The most significant was the drowning of Capel Celyn and the Tryweryn valley and the creation of Llyn Celyn for its water supply by the city of Liverpool in 1963. Of the Welsh members of Parliament 27 out of 36 voted against the Liverpool Corporation Bill when it was introduced in 1957. None voted for it but it was carried against what can be fairly described as the unanimous opposition of Welsh people. Trevor Fishlock, The Times journalist, wrote, 'the episode of Tryweryn was a traumatic one and is one of the keys to what has been happening in Wales in recent years. From it sprang a great anger and a hardening of resolve; for many men and women it was an awakening, the first indication that the values of Wales were in danger and were meaningless to the authorities in England' (Fishlock, 1972, 102). Or as one member of Cymdeithas Yr Iaith wrote, 'Daeth brwydr Tryweryn yn sumbol o'r frwydr dros hawliau iaith, hawliau cymdeithas a hawliau cenedl' (Tudur, 1989, 16). (In translation, 'The struggle for Tryweryn became a symbol of the struggle for the rights of the language, the rights of community and the rights of the nation'). The demonstrable arrogance and the crude manifestation of the English dominance of Wales built up a resentment which was released not in direct political terms, for Plaid Cymru in the late 1960s had only limited electoral success, but in renewed feelings of warmth for the language and by extension, to being Welsh. Perhaps this was because the language was an easily identifiable single issue as opposed to the complexities of political convictions, especially where, as has already been argued, in post-modern Wales formal political conflict seemed to arise over degree of administrative competence rather than ideology. But, in addition, the language can be seen as the only obvious remaining symbol of Welsh difference and identity so that even for non-Welsh speakers the language could be a symbol. And if they did not speak it, their children often could. The dramatic increases in the young speaking Welsh between 1981 and 1991 were clear evidence of a growing reaction. Six of the eight counties recorded increases in Welsh speakers of more than 30 per cent between 1981 and 1991; three counties recorded increases of double that proportion.

Together with Tryweryn perhaps the other most significant event was the creation in 1982 of a fourth Welsh language television channel, S4C as it became known. The channel had been promised by the Conservative Party in its manifesto but on coming into power in 1979 it prepared to renege on the promise. The threat by the president of Plaid Cymru, Gwynfor Evans, to fast to death and subsequent pressure from a group of prominent Welshmen anxious to avoid this brought a reversal of the decision. It was the opposite of Tryweryn, a victory for Wales over the English establishment, with the language the ultimate victor.

A clear indication of success in the battle for public opinion in the winning over of non-Welsh speakers, came in the poll conducted for the Welsh Language Board in 1996 (Welsh Language Board, 1996). It reported that 84 per cent of the sample who were Welsh-speaking supported the board's aim, 'to enable the language to become self-sustaining and secure as a medium of communication in Wales' and that 96 per cent of the Welsh-speakers and 94 per cent of the non-Welsh-speakers agreed that the numbers of Welsh speakers should be increased. Again, 94 per cent of the Welsh-speakers and 80 per cent of the non Welsh-speakers agreed that more opportunities to use the language should be provided (Welsh Language Board, 1996, 2-3). All these data underline how attitudes were won over and a firm basis for growth provided.

The discussion to date has been largely concerned with the fight to control public opinion. It was crucial that the success was turned into real gains in the field of education. The history of the development of

Welsh-medium education is far too large an issue to be dealt with effectively here. Suffice it to note that the first Welsh-medium primary school was established at Aberystwyth in 1939, although it was independent and did not come under the local education authority until 1951. The first local education authority Welsh-medium primary school was opened at Llanelli in 1947, while the first secondary school, Ysgol Glan Clwyd, was established at Rhyl by Flintshire County Council in 1956. The subsequent growth in such schools has had major consequence; so, too, has the determination of parents, especially in the urban areas of south Wales, to establish Welsh-medium nursery schools (Stevens, 1996). This latter movement began in 1949 at Maesteg and grew slowly at first but by 1970 had led to the establishment of some 60 ysgolion meithrin in all parts of Wales. Such has been the success of the initiative that by 1995 the number of nursery schools had reached 625, with a further 379 'mother and child' groups. Pertinently, a high proportion of the children attending these schools are from non Welsh-speaking homes. The University of Wales and other institutes of higher education in Wales have responded to the success of the schools. Since the late 1960s courses and degrees through the medium of Welsh have been offered at Aberystwyth and Bangor, as have teacher training programmes. The domain of education, which had been lost during the nineteenth century, has been effectively reclaimed. The inclusion of Welsh as a core subject in the national curriculum, and as a foundation subject in other schools in Wales (though that has subsequently been partly modified), was a real triumph for language activists. It is now possible to move from nursery education to post-doctoral research entirely within the Welsh language.

Equally, in the public domain the reinstatement of the language has reversed the restrictions first imposed at the Act of Union in 1536. That, too, has been a long and complex process, culminating in the Welsh Language Act of 1993. This not only ensured equality of Welsh with English before the law but set up a permanent Welsh Language Board 'to promote and facilitate the use of the Welsh language'. The Act states that every public body which provides services to the public in Wales or exercises statutory functions in relation to the provision by other public bodies of services to the public in Wales shall prepare a scheme specifying the measures it proposes to take as to the use of Welsh, 'so far as it is both appropriate in the circumstances and reasonably practical'. It ensures the right to use Welsh in the law courts, as long as due notice is given and dictates that all official forms and circulars are issued in Welsh. All this is overseen by the Language Board which in 1996 published *'A Strategy for the Welsh Language'* which sought to implement its remit to promote and facilitate the use of the Welsh language and ' to enable the Welsh language to be self-sustaining and secure as a medium of communication in Wales'. Twenty objectives are put forward and the Board's role and responsibility in each outlined, together with a comment on the task of realising them and a listing of partners in the process. The very existence of the strategy is evidence of the way in which attitudes to the language have been effectively transformed over the last quarter of a century.

If the language has become more and more accepted as the basis of Welsh identity and has support from speakers and non speakers alike, the traditional means of reproduction have been greatly weakened. The two domains in which Welsh remained most secure during the nineteenth century and the first half of the twentieth were the chapel and the home or the hearth (yr aelwyd). However, the late twentieth century has seen a great weakening of the influence of Nonconformist Christianity and the impact upon Welsh people of the secularism and consumerism of the western way of life. Above all, the Sunday school, which virtually saved the language through the use of the Welsh Bible, no longer functions as the provider of an education through the medium of Welsh. In addition, the instability of marriage, as well as the greater frequency of 'mixed marriages', which is a function of greater mobility, have undermined the effectiveness of the home as a transmitter of the language. Moreover, distance and inaccessibility once constituted the great defences of the language in the community but in the present century radio, and especially television, have brought English on to the hearth. Inaccessibility in an electronic age has no meaning.

The reduction in the numbers of all-Welsh-speaking households and the weakness of the hearth as the central strength of the language is evident. In 1991 as many as 68.6 per cent of households contained no children, although many of them were probably pensioners living alone. A total of 4.2 per cent have to be excluded because the children are under 3 and the language is not recorded by the census. A further 20.2 per cent of households contained children none of whom was Welsh-speaking. In only 6 per cent of households were there children all of whom spoke Welsh, forming a very limited base for the future. However, these figures, which relate to proportions of all households, are somewhat limited and it is more rewarding to turn to the separate groups. There the surprisingly high percentages of 9.8 and 49.4 are recorded for Welsh-speaking children in households where either none or only some of the adults were Welsh-speaking. This is an indication that the base for the future does not necessarily lie within the fractured households of contemporary Wales. One point of concern, however, was the extent to which the children of Welsh-speaking parents spoke Welsh. There was a clear decline in the amount of Welsh spoken across the family structure ranging from 91.1 per cent of the children between 3 and 15 where Welsh was spoken between husband and wife, through cohabiting parents, to single male and single female parents, where only 73.8 per cent of all the children spoke Welsh. Declining family stability suggests a smaller likelihood of all the offspring speaking Welsh.

The implications that follow from the decline of the chapel and the limitation of the family as the progenitors of the language are that other sources have arisen. These are the ones which have already received comment. The Welsh language schools, as well as facilities for adult learning, have become the real basis of a Welsh language renaissance. Their impact has been greatly supported by the Welsh language media. In brief, in contemporary Wales new or renewed bases for language reproduction have replaced the traditional and declining bases.

It would be wrong, however, to give the impression that resistance to this language renaissance does not exist. The survey for the Welsh Office already quoted certainly suggests a general backing but there are strident voices still raised, if not in direct opposition at least in a questioning mode. They are well represented in a quotation from Giggs and Pattie. 'There seems to be evidence of a cultural elitism among some Welsh-speaking Welsh people. It is heartening that proficiency in Britain's oldest language (hitherto long derided) provides dignity, social prestige and opportunity in Wales. At the same time it is profoundly disheartening that a few zealots can seriously assert that the English-speaking majority, who constitute 77.6 per cent of the Welsh-born residents in 1981…are 'not *really* Welsh'. Moreover, the problems are not simply those of proficiency in the Welsh language being touted as the essential qualification for Welsh nationality rather than mere nativity, which is deemed a sufficient qualification in the majority of countries: there are attendant cultural, political and economic implications'. (Giggs and Pattie, 1991, 29). These views can be taken to more extreme lengths as in a characteristic attack by Professor

Christie Davies of the Social Affairs Unit think tank as reported in the Western Mail for January 28, 1997 where the author of an article 'Loyalty Misplaced' is reported as calling for 'euthanasia of an already-dying language and immediate removal of bilingual signs' (Betts, 1997, 1). This re-echoes the view of Matthew Arnold quoted earlier in this paper.

The argument of those who agree with Giggs and Pattie but might not go quite as far as Davies is that out of the whole set of arrangements for the governance of Wales, including the existing national institutions such as the University, the Library and the Museum, and, of course, the Welsh Office and now the Welsh Assembly, a distinctive Welsh set of institutions will emerge from which the identity of Wales will be eventually derived, an identity which will be independent of language. This has a close link with Welsh academic Gwyn A. Williams's message in *'When was Wales?'*. 'Wales is an artefact which the Welsh produce: the Welsh make and remake Wales day by day and year after year' (Williams, G.A., 1979). Such a Wales will be more akin to Ireland where, although conventional obeisance is made to the Irish language, that language plays little real part in the national identity of the country. Such identity is derived from political freedom and independence and from the development of specific Irish institutions. In such a way a Welsh identity, based on distinctive institutions, will be more securely formed, and will include all the people who wish to call themselves Welsh and not only the limited number who are Welsh-speaking. In contrast to this view, which is characteristic of the intellectual middle class, Roberts reports from a study in Blaina and Nant-y-glo, 'in summary, there seems to be an emergent, stronger sense of cultural nationalism rather than a discernible trend towards national self-determination as a political demand' (Roberts, 1994, 89).

It is apparent that the conflict over language that characterised Wales in the past is not resolved. It spills over, of course, into the perennial conflict over whether Welshness depends on geographic location, personal association and will, or cultural identity as determined by language. It is because of the last possible determinant that the revival which has been here traced is still regarded with suspicion if not with downright opposition. The view that Wales would be better off without the language is one that is still extant and as vigorously advanced as in the time of Matthew Arnold. But the advantage as far as public opinion, or, otherwise, social and cultural reproduction is concerned, no longer rests exclusively with those who would seek to eliminate Welsh, and on that its revival has depended. Moreover, it is now primarily an urban and secular language better equipped to cope with the demands of the next century. But, if 'the concepts of language production and reproduction relate to three primary agencies - the family, education and community' (Nelde, Strubell and Williams 1996, 6), with the media being a further agency, this discussion has demonstrated that in the case of Welsh the family has become a much less certain agency than once it was while the conflict within the community, arbitrated by the media, will determine the course of education, a prime basis of contemporary reproduction.

Earlier in this chapter the trends denoting an apparent revival of Welsh, by examination of both numbers and proportion speaking, were set out. Subsequent discussion has attempted to highlight those elements which have been crucial in that revival and to lay out the impressive and extensive infrastructure which is now in place based on Welsh medium education and the place of Welsh in the core curriculum in Wales. Further support has been provided by a formal Welsh Language Act, in publishing through the backing of the Welsh Books Council, and in the broadcast media from BBC Radio Cymru and S4C.

What has been outlined and interpreted, however, is no more, and no less, than a stage in the process of the language's history. The crucial issue behind what success has been achieved, behind the foundation of the impressive infrastructure noted above, as indeed it was behind the long decline, has been access to power within the country and through it the ability to influence public opinion and attitudes. At the very heart of much of the discussion of language has been the notion of culture, and Welsh culture is often interpreted as an artefact in its own right. But it can be argued that culture itself is not a discrete and independent thing, 'an ontological given' (Mitchell, 1995), but rather a complex created in order to advance power bases. Mitchell contends that social theorists must 'dispense with the notion of an ontological culture and begin focusing instead on how the very idea of culture has been developed and deployed as a means of attempting to order, control and define "others" in the name of power and profit' (Mitchell, 1995, 104).

He maintains that 'culture...comes to signify artificial distinctiveness where in reality there is always contest and flux. What gets called "culture" is created through struggles by groups and individuals possessing radically different access to power' (Mitchell, 1995, 108).

If this be so, the whole of the language/ethnic identity complex is a reflection of the determination of the Welsh people to wrest control of their destiny from the hands of an uncaring and unsympathetic 'British' establishment where it was so long lodged. The slow creation of Welsh institutions in more recent times, to add to those of an earlier date, and from the relatively general such as the BBC National Orchestra of Wales, the Welsh National Opera or the National Botanic Garden, to the formation of a National Assembly, are all part of this process and a manifestation of a new confident and assertive identity. It is perhaps a dangerous assertion, but there surely can be little doubt that the whole of this movement was led by the struggle to maintain and grow the Welsh language. That view is backed by the widespread support for the language, even by those who do not speak it. It is also confirmed, possibly conversely, by the very narrow majority in favour of a Welsh Assembly. Given these favourable indications, and in the light of how we attempt to show how the Welsh have retained their identity in spite of all the problems over the years, it is pertinent to move to examine actual measures of identity.

Chapter 9
Measures of identity

There have been within the last decade some studies that purport to provide a measure of identity. Three of these can be examined here. The first is the response to the question on ethnicity in the 2001 census, the second to the similar question in the 2001 Labour Area Force Survey. These are shown in Table 9.1 together with comparable data for the percentages Welsh-speaking and born in Wales. The third comes from a study by the Centre for Research into Elections and Social Trends and is presented in a paper by Robert Andersen entitled *'National identity and independence attitudes: minority nationalism in Scotland and Wales'*. It is based on the returns from a random sample of some 1,255 over eighteen year olds conducted partly by phone and partly by post. It is based on what the author calls the 'Moreno scale' where respondents are invited to classify themselves as Welsh and not British, More Welsh than British, Equally Welsh and British, More British than Welsh, or British not Welsh. The returns for Wales are shown in Table 9.2.

A further source is considered. This is a series of reports from Social Identification and Social Action in Wales (SISAW). These are different being not numerical in nature but consisting of what can be called content analysis of interviews with a limited number of Welsh residents, as well as speeches by public figures. One particular paper by Livingstone, Spears and Manstead will be used, entitled *'The Language of Change? Characterisations of in-group social position, threat, and the deployment of distinct group attitudes'* (2009).

The 2001 census question asked was, 'What is your ethnic group?', giving the choice - White, Mixed, Asian or Asian British, Black or Black British and Chinese or Other. Under the White heading the possibilities presented were British, Irish, or Any Other White Background. In light of the discussion of culture and ethnicity at the outset of this volume a brief comment must be made on this list of choices for in any *ethnic* sense 'black' or 'white' have no meaning. More to the point of this book there was no 'Welsh' identity tick box. This omission was compounded by the offer of a 'Scottish' choice in the census form for Scotland.

There was a protest in Wales but the Office for National Statistics refused to act on the grounds that it would be too expensive to make an alteration at a late stage and in any case there had been no objections when the forms were circulated for comment before being finalised. A campaign was launched to persuade those filling in the forms to enter 'Welsh' in the 'Any other white background' tick box. The subsequent data are shown in Table 9.1 where the proportions of those choosing to declare themselves Welsh are entered.

Table 9.1
Ethnicity: Census 2001 and Labour Area Force Survey 2001

Unitary Authority	Per cent Welsh speaking	Per cent Welsh born	Welsh Identity Census 2001	Welsh Identity Labour Survey	Welsh Identity Per cent Welsh born
Blaenau Gwent	9.1	92.1	12.0	85.2	2
Bridgend	10.6	84.7	15.8	79.1	2
Caerphilly	10.9	89.9	15.5	82.5	3
Cardiff	10.9	74.9	13.2	66.5	4
Carmarthenshire	50.1	80.1	23.4	76.0	1
Ceredigion	51.8	58.6	21.8	66.2	1
Conwy	29.2	54.0	12.1	71.3	5
Denbighshire	26.1	57.9	10.6	50.3	3
Flintshire	14.1	51.1	5.8	43.3	5
Gwynedd	68.7	69.8	26.8	71.3	1
Merthyr Tydfil	10.0	92.0	16.2	87.0	1
Monmouthshire	9.0	61.3	6.9	54.3	5
Neath/Port Talbot	17.8	89.5	17.0	82.7	2
Newport	9.6	81.1	9.0	69.6	5
Pembrokeshire	21.5	68.7	13.1	60.5	4
Powys	20.8	55.6	12.6	56.2	3
Rhondda Cynon Taf	12.3	89.9	16.5	84.3	2
Swansea	13.2	82.1	15.3	73.0	4
Torfaen	10.7	85.5	9.8	75.8	3
Vale of Glamorgan	11.1	75.7	12.8	69.9	3
Wrexham	14.4	71.9	9.4	67.1	2
Ynys Mon	59.9	67.6	19.4`	60.1	3
Wales	20.5	75.4	14.4	69.2	-

Note: The Labour Force Survey also returned Welsh identity related to being Welsh born. Unfortunately this appears only as a map and is simply stated as not available as a table. In consequence the last column is derived from the map and places each county in a category 1 to 5 as can be derived from the map with 1 being the highest percentage and 5 the lowest.

The census returns are largely as expected. The Welsh speaking areas of north and west Wales record the highest proportions, although they are comparatively low at little more than twenty per cent, with the highest being Gwynedd with 26.8 per cent. Interestingly, although there is a clear relationship with the language there is no such link with place of birth. Some of the authorities with the highest proportions of Welsh born recorded low proportions declaring themselves to be Welsh. Thus, Blaenau Gwent with 92.1 per cent Welsh-born returned only 12 per cent as of Welsh identity and Merthyr Tydfil with 92.0 per cent Welsh-born only 16.2 per cent. For Wales as a whole only 14.4 per cent were sufficiently determined to register themselves as Welsh.

Table 9.2
National Identity in Wales.
Reponses to the Moreno identity scale (after Andersen)

Welsh not British	17.9
More Welsh than British	20.2
Equally Welsh and British	39.0
More British than Welsh	8.3
British not Welsh	14.6

These are percentage of answers to the question, 'Which of the following best describes how you see yourself'.

If the figures recorded by the Labour Force Survey are examined, there emerges a startling contrast for it totally reverses the Census data. In that survey respondents were given the choices of identifying themselves as Welsh, English, Scottish, Irish, British or any other national identity. The highest proportions recording themselves as Welsh are found in the former iron-working and coal mining areas of south Wales. Merthyr Tydfil returns 87 per cent, Blaenau Gwent 85.2 per cent and Rhondda Cynon Taff 84.3 per cent. The highest of the traditionally Welsh-speaking areas is Carmarthenshire with 76 per cent. Even in Torfaen, where only 2.5 per cent speak Welsh, 75.8 per cent returned themselves as Welsh, virtually the same as Carmarthenshire where at the 2001 census 50.1 per cent claimed to be Welsh-speaking. In Ceredigion, where 59.1 per cent were Welsh-speaking in 2001, only 66.2 per cent recorded themselves as Welsh in the Labour Force Survey. Perhaps as a proviso, it has to be noted that the census asked for 'ethnic group', the Labour Force Survey for 'national identity'. But it is difficult to see that any great difference would result from these two different ways of asking the same basic question.

The explanation for these anomalies is at first seemingly straightforward. As Chapter 7 showed, whereas the rural counties have experienced substantial immigration during the past decades the same was not true of the older industrial areas which were manifestly a less desirable target for migrants. The validity of this is confirmed by the column giving place of birth and by the last column where identity is associated with place of birth. Whereas 92.1 per cent of the population of Blaenau Gwent were Welsh born and 92 per cent in Merthyr Tydfil, only 58.6 per cent of Ceredigion's population were born in Wales. It is the impact of these 'outsiders' which leads to the apparent anomaly of the areas with the lowest proportion of Welsh speakers returning the highest proportions identifying themselves as Welsh. But there is more to it than that simple conclusion. Why did not the industrial areas give similarly high figures at the census? Why did not populations there write themselves in as Welsh? Clearly, the answer can only be explained by commitment. Faced with the necessity to write in an identity only those massively committed to being Welsh responded. Indeed, it is possible that many outside the hothouse of 'national' feeling might not have even been aware of the situation. Conviction as to being Welsh, therefore, was apparently very much lower in the industrial areas. The writing in of identity was a declaration of passion, of belief in language and culture.

The return in the Labour Force Survey was, therefore, more a response to location and an acceptance of place, with the reality of Welshness probably related to more superficial aspects, such as support for rugby or soccer teams. That so many declared themselves as Welsh, however, does reflect a basic conviction of Welsh identity. A footnote to the survey adds that a logistic regression analysis was conducted which showed that the factors independently associated with having a Welsh identity were country of birth, Welsh language ability, unitary authority areas, educational qualifications, socio-economic class and age. The survey states that: 'Those with fewer educational qualifications were more likely to report a Welsh identity. For example, three quarters of people with no qualifications said their national identity was Welsh (75 per cent) compared with only half of those with a degree or equivalent qualification (51 per cent). Similarly, people in routine occupations were more likely than those in the higher managerial or professional socio-economic class to say that their national identity was Welsh. These findings may seem at odds with the contention that much of the success of the language has depended on the rise to higher social status of opinion formers. But they are a minority seeking to exercise control. The language relation in the census data is as expected, while in the Labour Force data the association of the less educated and the lower social order is linked to the high returns of Welsh identity in the industrial areas and the general assumption of higher status of in-migrants moving to jobs in Wales. (These figures predate the inflow of populations from Eastern Europe.)

The upshot of this discussion is that it is possible to suggest that there are contrasted forms of Welshness in Wales. One is closely connected with the language and the culture associated with it. Its members are probably more aware of Welsh history, and identity rests on a commitment to language and the traditions based on it. On the other hand there is a Welsh identity which is essentially locationally based, that is it is a more direct response to place, possibly to accent rather than language, but of necessity one developed over some time. It is much more the product of industrialisation and all the concomitant features. All that is, however, sufficient to engender a belief in being Welsh rather than British, although one suspects that the Welsh element is subservient to the industrial culture. Many of the characteristics of south Wales in particular are more related to the camaraderie of mining and steel working rather than to Wales as such. Wales is blended into a conglomerate of social features.

The data in Figure 9.2 from the survey by Andersen would seem to confirm the conclusions drawn from the census and Labour Area Force Survey. Only 17.9 per cent declared themselves to be Welsh not British, a proportion very similar to the 14.4 percent who wrote in a Welsh identity in the 2001 census. The largest proportion chose the median position of being equally Welsh and British, an indication possibly of that lack of conviction among non-Welsh speakers suggested by the earlier data. The assumption can be made that the 14.6 percent who said that they were British and not Welsh were made up largely of recent in-migrants, those who have lowered the proportion of Welsh speakers in those areas away from the industrial heartland. There are of course, no cross references to other socio-economic data so that only assumptions can be made.

From the paper by Livingstone et al. other interesting findings emerge.

Welsh speakers generally considered the language a necessary part of Welshness. More interesting is the attitude of non-Welsh speakers. As might be expected the responses ranged from an acceptance of the language criterion and an admission that the language should be learned, through an agreement that the language is an essential symbol of identity, even if is not spoken and there is no intention to learn it, to a complete rejection that the ability to speak language is an essential part of identity. The real problem in that last attitude is what replaces language and there was very little in the way of convincing criteria. There were suggestions of an economic nature – Wales is primarily socialist - and of a locational and political nature – 'We are not English'. But these seem to carry little in the way of clear conviction. This is reflected in the extracts from a speech by Rhodri Morgan made in 2005 to inaugurate the first Wales Identity Day. He is quoted as saying, 'It is always surprising the different views that people have of Wales and what makes them Welsh......These views and perceptions create a rich and vibrant tapestry, which when woven together captures the essence of Wales and what it means to be Welsh. But no matter what the differences, we have a national heritage that binds together and makes us proud of this country'. The authors comment, 'the action impulse in this construction of Welshness is on the articulation and celebration of different attributes as facets of a rich identity, rather than on deploying any of them as a means of managing a threatened identity (Livingstone et al, 12). But the crucial issue is what exactly makes up the 'heritage'. There little is offered other than references to the language and literature and to writing in English, together with industrialisation and landscape. It is pertinent to add here the gloom of the Welsh tourist industry at the lack of specifically Welsh heritage features. There are no easily exploited equivalents of Bannockburn or the tartan.

The conclusions from this chapter are hardly satisfactory. Clearly the qualification for identity ranges from a total association with language and its associated culture to one which is primarily locational. 'We are Welsh because we live in Wales'. But attempts at the identification of associated, crucial traits provide but vague answers. What has to be recognized is that such a wide divergence exists and that resolution is the needed future step.

In this chapter as in others the matter of criteria other than language which are characteristic of Wales has been raised. There has been one, however, widely recognized even beyond Wales and that is the so-called

Welsh Sunday. It was widely known because on Sunday public houses were closed and alcoholic drinks unavailable, a condition which irked visitors to Wales, it was a feature which the tourist industry did not support! This one clear criterion of difference is worth reviewing.

Chapter 10

An element of culture: The demise of the Welsh Sunday

One of the traditional characteristics of Wales has been the so-called Welsh Sunday, Bible-black according to Dylan Thomas. Until recent times the fourth commandment was closely observed. Food was prepared on Saturday night so that there was a minimum of work on the Sabbath; children were allowed no toys, only 'good' books were read; there was a complete prohibition of sensual pleasures; the day was devoted to the worship of God. That alcohol should be consumed at any time was abhorrent to the devout chapelgoer; that it should be consumed on Sunday in premises open for that purpose was well nigh intolerable.

The Sunday Closing Act was a private members bill introduced during Gladstone's second ministry and received its second reading on May 4th, 1881. Great stress was laid during the debate on the wide measure of support that the Sunday closing movement had attracted from all parts of Wales, north and south, urban and rural, a support which was generally estimated at being at least three to one. It was also argued that the support transcended all the religious allegiances of the time. But there were clearly two bases of backing. The first, as indicated above, was religious Nonconformity, with its ascetic views on alcohol in general and its insistence on Sunday observance. It does need to be added that the proliferation of taverns and public houses that had characterised the growth of industry had led to serious social problems and the movement was a reaction to those problems. The second basis lay in the national aspirations which were being increasingly articulated in the late nineteenth century and which have already been discussed. The Sunday Closing Act was the first occasion for some 250 years that Wales had been treated as a separate unit. Gladstone himself during the debate referred to the shabby treatment that Wales had received in the past and the desirability of the government's discovering whether there was a distinct Welsh opinion. But above all on the occasion of the second reading he referred to Wales as, 'after all a country with a people of its own, with traditions of its own and especially religious feelings and associations of its own' (Parliamentary Papers, 1881). To hear this English high church zealot admitting this much must have sounded a significant triumph for Welsh members. All this meant that the Act acquired a symbolism far wider than its reference to Sunday opening. It became a marker of Welsh difference when few others existed. In relation to what was noted at the beginning of Chapter 3, it must be added that the Act did not include Monmouthshire which was not affected until 1915 when as part of war time legislation Sunday closing was extended to cover the county.

In a parallel example Andrew Sinclair in his book, *Prohibition. An Era of Excess*, demonstrates that there was a lot more to the Eighteenth Amendment of the USA constitution than a simple conflict between 'wets and 'drys'. On this issue, he writes, the old traditional, rural and, oddly enough, Anglo-Saxon America found an issue that could focus its discontent with the new industrial, cosmopolitan and urban America. 'This worship of a whitewashed past, this fear of a defeated future, made prohibition a crusade of the old Eden against the devils of the new Babylon. The Eighteenth Amendment was one of the last victories of the village pulpit against the factory proletariat, of the Corn Belt against the conveyor belt' (Sinclair, 1962). There is no direct relation between prohibition and the Welsh Sunday but the American example is introduced to demonstrate that acts of government can have a cultural resonance that is far beyond their immediate purpose.

Table 10.1

Polls on Sunday Opening 1961 and 1968. Percentages

County	1961		1968	
	Dry	Poll	Dry	Poll
Anglesey	76	57	66	57
Merioneth	76	65	66	60
Cardigan	74	62	64	54
Caernarfon	71	60	62	50
Carmarthen	67	61	62	50
Pembroke	58	46	43	43
Montgomery	57	58	41	54
Denbigh	53	54	40	48
Brecon	47	53	31	37
Radnor	42	55	23	51
Glamorgan	40	41	33	18
Flint	39	50	20	36
Cardiff	38	34	19	20
Swansea	38	45	29	20
Merthyr	34	52	23	24
Monmouth	28	40	18	19
Newport	27	34	No Poll	

By the second half of the twentieth century a strong reaction to the Sunday Closing Act had developed. Closure was hardly in keeping with the liberalism which marked the 1960s and it was regarded as particularly irksome by publicans, hoteliers and all engaged in the tourist industry. Local opinion polls had been held, the most significant in 1961, but the formal campaign against the Act was led by the Seven Day Opening Council and the Retail Licensed Trade in Wales and Monmouthshire.

Table 10.2
Polls on Sunday Opening 1975, 1982 and 1989. Percentages

District	1975		1982		1989	
	Dry	Poll	Dry	Poll	Dry	Poll
Dwyfor	66	60	59	53	57	40
Ceredigion	59	49	52	44	48	41
Meirionydd	57	59	47	56	39	48
Carmarthen	55	51	49	45	42	31
Arfon	55	48	48	43	37	31
Ynys Môn	54	51	47	48	36	35
Dinefwr	48	50	37	40	38	26
Llanelli	38	45	26	35	30	19
Glyndŵr	36	48	27	39	NP	
Aberconwy	34	50	26	32	24	22
Colwyn	32	41	30	28	25	22
Lliw Valley	31	30	NP		NP	
Montgomery	29	45	21	38	NP	
Preseli	28	43	24	32	21	23
South Pembs.	22	42	NP		NP	
Afan	2	22	NP		NP	
Rhuddlan	19	33	NP		NP	
Wrexham	16	39	11	31	NP	
Neath	NP		21	24	NP	
Taff-Ely	NP		NP		22	12
Cardiff	NP		NP		21	9
Newport	NP		NP		19	25

Note: NP in Figures 10,1, 2, and 3 indicate that there was no poll. The first referendum had taken place in 1961 and the second in 1968. They were county based but after 1968 following changes in local government areas the poll was based on the new districts.

Their activities resulted in the passing of the 1964 Licensing Act. Under that Act local opinion polls were in future to be held as to whether public houses could open on Sundays every seven years, if they were demanded by 500 people who were eligible to vote in local elections.

Table 10.3
Areas voting 'Dry' 1961-1996

1961	1968	1975	1982	1989	1996
Anglesey	Anglesey	Ynys Môn	Dwyfor	Dwyfor	None
Merioneth	Merioneth	Meirionydd	Ceredigion		
Cardigan	Cardigan	Ceredigion			
Caernarfon	Caernarfon	Dwyfor			
Carmarthen	Carmarthen	Arfon			
Pembroke		Carmarthen			
Montgomery					
Denbigh					

The three tables, 10.1, 10.2 and 10.3, need very little exegesis. They demonstrate the way in which the closing of public houses on Sunday was progressively rejected almost directly in line with the proportion of Welsh speakers, virtually like the stripping of the skins of an onion. Successive layers of adherence to the Act were peeled away over the septennial referenda until by 1996 all had abandoned Sunday closing. In that process the closure was most strongly and longer supported by those areas where Welsh was most spoken and where Calvinistic Methodism dominated the religious scene. The poll in 1961 divided Wales into two in a direct replica of Y Gymry Gymraeg and Y Gymry Ddi-Gymraeg. Successive declines in the area covered paralleled the decline of the language but whereas in recent years the language has markedly revived the opposite has been true of Sunday closing. By the second half of the twentieth century a strong reaction against the Act had developed.

There were a number of reasons. The first was the general advance of liberal attitudes, which characterised the whole of Britain in the 1960s. The rejection of old conformities was part of the ethos of the times: restrictions of any sort were anathema. The second was the decline of religious beliefs and the rise of a material secularism. Max Boyce's song – 'the miners' baths are a supermarket now' - might well have said, too, that the chapel was a second home! Another powerful reason was the lobbying of the tourist industry which considered that the lack of drinking facilities in Wales on Sundays was a drag on the development of tourism at a time when it was being seen as one of the main growth points of the Welsh economy. This is a point which can be shown from the polling statistics. At the time the detailed figures from the polling centres were regarded as strictly confidential, presumably because of the internal conflicts which they might have generated. I was, however, able to obtain some data, although I was asked to respect its confidentiality. Some forty years later, I assume that the restrictions need no longer be observed. In 1968 the 'Dry' vote in Merioneth by district was, Edeyrnion Rural District 68 per cent; Bala Urban District and Penllŷn Rural District 77 per cent; Towyn Urban District, which included the parish of Pennal, 54 per cent; Dolgellau Urban district, plus a set of neighbouring parishes, 70 per cent; Deudraeth Rural District 66 per cent; Barmouth Urban District, plus some neighbouring five parishes, 47 per cent. Merioneth as a whole, of course, remained 'dry' in 1968, but one area did actually vote 'wet' and that was Barmouth which was the urban core of the tourist trade in the county and Tywyn nearly followed it. The decline in the influence of the chapel, the throwing off of the restrictions of an earlier less tolerant era and the demands of economic growth via tourism, all brought the one hundred years of Sunday closing to an end. No area voted to stay dry in 1996 and the Government undertook to repeal the Act. It took a further seven years until 2003 before the Licensing Act put an end to the system of seven year referenda.

This elimination of what once had been a veritable icon of the Welsh does raise problems. That it was an icon is surely true. For in the perception of many outsiders the stereotypical Welshman, and the gender is purposefully used, is still a chapel-going, hymn-singing miner, although the mines have long since closed and with them many of the chapels. They are the symbols of a past era. But more to the point of present reality, if one significant element of identity has been lost how secure are some others? Also under threat, for example, is the tradition of choral singing as it was taught in the chapels, in the 'ysgol gân', the singing practice, often held after the evening service. Certainly, there is every indication of a weakening of that tradition. Part-singing is no longer widely practised and the old hymns sung at rugby internationals have been replaced by songs in English such as 'Delilah' that have no link with Welsh culture. Even Cwm Rhondda, the one remaining, is sung in an English version. Before long the Reverend Eli Jenkins will not be able thank God that we are a musical nation.

Given the loss of such a significant icon one naturally turns to others which might be under threat and the most immediate and obvious is the language. Throughout this book the language has been put forward as the matrix which binds together all the other elements that contribute to Welshness, which can be regarded as a conglomerate collected and unified by the language. Perforce one has to ask the question of the extent to which the language is an essential, especially given that three quarters of the people do not speak it. Moreover, ethnic distinction does not necessarily rest on language. The Scots certainly do not depend on Gaelic for their sense of difference. Lallans, while recognised as a language, is no more than a version of northern English. Scottish identity has a much greater dependency on its long standing institutions and an independence and unity which lasted until the beginning of the eighteenth century. It is an over simplification to argue that Scotland retained its institutions but lost its language while Wales lost its institutions but retained its language, but the cultural matrices of the countries do offer strong contrasts.

These speculations bring us nearer to a consideration of the contemporary bases of identity but before embarking on that it is appropriate to review the role of the capital city which across the whole of the western world has had such a crucial role in the preservation of identity.

Chapter 11
The Capital City and Welsh identity

In 1939 Mark Jefferson published a paper entitled '*The Law of the Primate City*'. One of the main concerns of urban geographers had been to establish if there were any order or system in the sizes of towns within a country; and here, it must be admitted, we are considering countries not ethnic groups. The accepted answer was that developed by Walther Christaller. His central place theory argued that towns were ordered into distinctive ranks forming what he called an urban hierarchy (Carter, 1995, 25). Jefferson's paper disputed that theory and maintained that the common pattern throughout the world was one characterised by the total dominance of one city, the primate city, with a long array of settlements smaller in size below. Generally, it is apparent that the law of the primate city holds mainly in pre-industrial societies, as is clearly demonstrated in Table 11.1.

Table 11.1
Populations of London and the next largest English cities 1600-1801

(After Daunton, 1978)

Date	London	Next largest city	Multiplier
1600	250,000	15,000 (Norwich)	17
1750	655,000	50,000 (Bristol)	13
1801	960,000	84,000 (Manchester)	11
1851	2,400,000	376,000 (Liverpool)	6

In 1600 London was seventeen times the size of the next largest city. Even in 1851 it was six times the nearest in size. In 1851 Paris accounted for 19.5 per cent of the urban population of France while the next ten cities of over 50,000 together only made up 16 per cent. But there was more to primacy than economic dominance, as indeed the term suggests. These cities epitomised the whole culture of the countries of which they were the capitals. 'Primate' and 'capital' have much in common. Paris in that sense was France, it epitomised the French way of life, and to such an extent that much later a book could be written called '*Paris and the French Desert*' emphasising the total dominance of the capital and primate city. The discussion of ethnicity and territory in Chapter 3 made very clear the significance of Jerusalem to the Israelis.

If we turn to Wales and look for a primate city, it is obvious that no such city existed. All the Welsh traditions were primarily rural. As

Giraldus Cambrensis asserted in the twelfth century, 'the Welsh people do not live in towns'. The town was an Anglo-Norman intrusion, although ultimately as we have tried to show in Chapter 7, effectively taken over by the Welsh. It was not until 1955 that Cardiff was made the capital of Wales, its primate city. We have recorded the populations of London and Paris in the early nineteenth century. At the first census in 1801 Cardiff had a population of 1870 and was only 21st in the size ranking of Welsh towns. To give some relevant comparisons, in 1851 the population of Edinburgh was 194,000 and Dublin 263,000. Cardiff's population was 18,350. There is no need to prolong this discussion for it is manifest that Cardiff is a parvenu, a late comer into the rank of larger towns and even then of no great magnitude. If we consider the traditional culture of Wales and all the elements that compose it, Cardiff has played no predominant part in its evolution and the development of its character. Its later dominance in Wales was largely the creation of the export of coal and of industry. In these circumstances a rather different question arises and that is whether by its size, consequent upon its economic role, has Cardiff been able at this late date to assume the role of the primate city. It has been designated the capital of Wales but is the part it has played and is playing of any relevance to the question with which this book started, the nature of Welsh identity?

There are two aspects to the role of the capital. The first is the extent to which Cardiff has collected the physical manifestations of Welsh separateness, those institutions and buildings that the movement towards the greater independence of Wales has generated. The second is the degree to which Cardiff has moved to become part of the beating heart of Wales, close to the driving elements of its cultural autonomy. The two aspects are obviously linked but need to be treated separately.

Although only formally designated as the capital in 1955 Cardiff has assembled an impressive array of the external markers of Welsh distinctiveness. The earliest was probably the National Museum of Wales founded in 1903, with the royal charter granted in 1907. At that time there was sufficient doubt about the dominance of Cardiff that the National Library of Wales, granted a charter at the same date, was located at Aberystwyth. Even so, Welsh institutions as they emerged in the last century were located in Cardiff, for example the Welsh Department of the Board of Education in 1907. The main run of foundations dates from after the Second World War and the lead was the creation of a Secretary of State for Welsh Affairs in 1964 after the founding of the Welsh Office in 1963. This was the forerunner of the wide array of public functions, some shifted from elsewhere in Wales, which were located in Cardiff. The apotheosis was, of course, the establishment of the Welsh Assembly after the narrow vote in favour of devolution in 1997. With all its various departments, and the civil service associated, Cardiff became the anchor of Welsh political, economic and social affairs. The Assembly building has become the physical representation of these functions.

Along with the Assembly one can list a series of national institutions. The BBC and ITV fix the predominance of the media. Even the Welsh language service, S4C, is located in Cardiff. The BBC National Orchestra of Wales and Welsh National Opera represent the contemporary face of Welsh music. Also in Cardiff is the Royal Welsh College of Music and Drama, described in the *Encyclopaedia of Wales* as 'Wales's only specialist centre for professional training in music and drama'. There is no National Art Gallery but plans for the creation of such an institution are closely linked to Cardiff. The Welsh Folk Museum at St Fagans just outside Cardiff has mutated through various titles to become the Museum of Welsh History. In other fields the Millennium Stadium is the basis for both international rugby and sometimes soccer. There is little purpose in a further narration of organisations centred in Cardiff, the listing is surely sufficient to make the point that in relation to the first aspect noted above the city has indeed collected over the past century or more the bulk of the physical manifestations of Wales as an independent entity.

There is an element of superficiality in simply setting out these facts, and a deeper examination will reveal that it is a word with some resonance. Let us take another example as an indicator. The University of Wales was for long regarded as one of the unifying and representative institutions of the country, a hallmark of its identity with its Registry in Cathays Park in Cardiff. But the association with Wales was not in keeping with the ambitions of what was the University College of South Wales and Monmouthshire or even the University of Wales, Cardiff as it later became styled. It baulked, apparently, at being merely a college, in spite of the fact that the most distinguished universities in Britain, Oxford, Cambridge and London, are made up of constituent colleges. But even more humiliating to the College was the conjunction with Wales; almost it would seem in line with the aversions which have been recorded earlier in this book. So Wales had to go, and the University of Cardiff was created. I present this as a symbol of an attitude which appears again and again. Nothing illustrates that better than the vote in 1997 on devolution and on that very Assembly which has been paramount in much of Cardiff's recent growth. At the referendum on devolution only 44.4 per cent in Cardiff voted in favour of devolution and 55.6 per cent against. The complete irony follows that the city which rejected any measure of devolution has become the centre where the devolved powers are located and exercised.

All the institutions located in Cardiff have some element of schizophrenia. For there is certainly a possible case to be made that some of those institutions located in the city seem to belong primarily to the city rather than the nation and the people. Cardiff, it can be argued, has ambitions to be an international city more than it wants to be the epitome of things Welsh. It is only Welsh where some advantage accrues. This is possibly an extreme view, which would be greatly contested by Cardiffians, but I am sure it will have some resonance with many outside the capital city.

The problem of gauging how close Cardiff lies to the real heart of Wales has the obvious difficulty we have met with so often in this study of defining any criteria. Once again, in consequence, one falls back on the language. However much many would disagree with its being so employed it is at least a measurable factor. Table 11.2 shows the numbers and proportions speaking Welsh from 1901 when the present definition of those over the age of three was adopted. It must be stressed that these data refer to different definitions of the city, for its extent has changed over time (see note below), and to small differences in the interpretation of Welsh speakers. Interpretation has, therefore, to be cautious but even so the rapid and substantial increases in both numbers and in the percentages are unmistakable. In 1987 my colleague, Professor John Aitchison, and I published a paper entitled 'The Welsh Language in Cardiff. A quiet revolution'. This was the first occasion on which attention was drawn to the noticeable and significant increases in the Welsh speakers in Cardiff. Since that date the trend has not only been maintained but palpably increased.

Table 11.2
The Numbers and Proportions of Welsh Speakers in Cardiff 1901-2001

Date	Number	Percentage
1901	12395	8.1
1911	11315	6.7
1921	9442	5.0
1931	10862	5.1
1951	9623	4.2
1961	11545	4.7
1971	12930	4.9
1981	14245	5.9
1991	17171	6.4
2001	32504	11.1

Note: The communities of Creigiau and Pentyrch were added to Cardiff under the 1996 Boundary Review. That explains some of the significant increase.

The causes for this 'revolution', as we called it, lie in the transformation of the economy of south Wales, already partly discussed in Chapter 8 on 'Regeneration'. The area of old decaying heavy industry in the USA had been called 'the rust belt' and such a description could well be applied to south Wales by the second half of the twentieth century. Margaret Thatcher, with her attempts to revitalise Britain and to drag it kicking and screaming into the post modern era, was largely responsible for the changes. New Labour continued those policies and added partially devolved government and a Welsh Assembly. All this gave a new dynamic to Cardiff, which, building on its former role as a coal exporter and the managerial centre of south Welsh industry, became a transactional city where services dominated and employment in administration, the media, finance and financial services as well as wholesaling and retailing have became predominant. It is significant that it has been suggested that Cardiff should become the centre for a Welsh Stock Exchange.

It is oddly ironic that Mrs Thatcher who had no particular love for Wales, even if she was aware that it existed, and in John Redwood as Secretary of State made what must surely be the most bizarre appointment ever to a British cabinet, nevertheless promoted policies that revitalised the language. In Cardiff the new openings in employment, especially in administration and in the media, brought into the city young people, many graduates of the University of Wales and very often Welsh speaking seeking work in their own country where before they might have been forced to emigrate. As they moved to the city they set up new demands for the language to be used, especially for the education of their children and Welsh-medium education developed apace in Cardiff.

These changes can be demonstrated from two sources. The first is the patterns of immigration to Cardiff. Data from the 2001 census is shown in Table 11.3

Table 11.3
In-migration to South Glamorgan 1991 Census

	Percent Migration	Percent Welsh Speaking
Clwyd	0.9	33.3
Dyfed	3.8	39.6
Gwent	5.6	5.7
Gwynedd	1.3	60.9
Mid Glam.	15.2	8.7
Powys	0.8	16.9
West Glam.	3.0	16.2
External	69.3	4.1

At the date of the census some 6.4 per cent of the population of Cardiff spoke Welsh so that of all the counties sending migrants to Cardiff only one, Gwent, failed to send a higher proportion of Welsh speakers than that already at Cardiff. Migration served to increase the number of Cardiff's Welsh speakers, although the high proportion from outside Wales has to be borne in mind.

Patterns of migration were reported in a Bulletin of the Statistical Directorate of the National Assembly. The figures are based on the National Health Service patient register data system where there are some reliability problems and are presented for aggregated regions. The bulletin states that although the south west of Wales showed a net inflow it nevertheless 'experienced a net loss of migrants to the south east, with an average of 140 more people per year migrating out than in. The net out migration from the south west to Cardiff was double this (280 people per year) as the three other authorities in the south east experienced a net outflow to the south west' (Welsh Assembly, Statistical Directorate, 2006, 5). It states 'Despite having a net inflow of migrants from north, mid and the south west, the south east had a net outflow...due to a large outflow...to the neighbouring Valleys region' (Welsh Assembly, Statistical Directorate, 2006, 6). Here is also the evidence of how Cardiff gathers migrants from all the Welsh regions, except for the Valleys, with the outflow to that area probably due to the cost of housing pushing out families from Cardiff, part of the same process. It is significant that for the 16-24 age group the flow was reversed with more moving into Cardiff. All this is evidence of the movement into Cardiff of significant numbers from the other regions of Wales and of the contribution those made to the Welsh-speaking proportions in the city.

The other source for an indication of these changes is in the social composition of the communities in the city. Table 11.4 lists the communities with the highest proportion in managerial and professional occupations alongside those communities with the highest percentages of Welsh speakers in 2001.

Table 11.4
Communities with the highest percentages of Social Grade AB and those with the highest percentages of Welsh speakers

Communities with highest social grade	Communities with highest percentage Welsh speakers
Lisvane	Pentyrch
Radyr	Creigiau
Creigiau	Canton
Cyncoed	Radyr
Pentyrch	Llandaff
Pontprennau	Riverside
Llandaff	Whitchurch

Note: Social Grade AB is defined as Higher and intermediate managerial, administrative professional, persons.

There is no complete agreement between the two columns but taking into account the impact of the student population on the Welsh proportion there is a sufficiently common occurrence between them to indicate a relation between higher social grade and Welsh speech. This is not in keeping with expectations. Thus, Glyn Williams writes in relation to Gwynedd, 'there have been profound developments of branch plant and new manufacturing industries. The most obvious feature of such development is that if the employment decisions for both manufacturing and retail are made outside Wales at head office, most of the higher level managerial or professional posts will be held by in-migrants. On the other hand, if the objective is the search for cheap labour, the proletarian labour will be local. That is, we envisage two different labour markets for different class locations...There is a heavy under-representation of Welsh speakers in the top four official socio-economic groups used in the census tabulations (G. Williams, 1986, 187). We have noted that condition in Chapter 9 on measures of identity but the data we have presented here demonstrates that Cardiff shows the reverse of this situation and this is due to those in-migrant Welsh speakers taking up posts in Cardiff in those very professional occupations that make up the highest social grades. The upshot is that Cardiff has now possibly the closest association with the language of Wales that it has ever had, which at least makes its claim as the life-spring of the Welsh more feasible.

After this somewhat discursive consideration of the role of Cardiff it is necessary to arrive at some conclusions. Cardiff is not and never has been a primate city. The cathedral of the patron saint is at St Davids; the first festival of music and poetry, the eisteddfod, was held at Cardigan and is now peripatetic; the most significant early assembly was held at Machynlleth; the first institute of higher learning was at Aberystwyth, which notably claims to be the cultural capital. For what it is worth to persons of sense and sensibility, since it re-echoes the presentation of Edward II to a conquered Wales, the installation of the Prince of Wales takes place at Caernarfon. In short, Cardiff has not played a leading part in the formative processes of the ethnic people called the Welsh.

It follows that any significance that Cardiff has in relation to being Welsh must have been derived in little more than the last century. The review we have carried out of that period suggest a complete schizophrenia. Situated in the extreme southern corner and removed from the heart of what is commonly regarded as Welsh Wales Cardiff can be regarded as predominantly the metropolis of the south east. It may be the capital of Wales, but it is not the capital of the Welsh. That is perhaps a harsh view for as we have suggested there is a two-way split in the city's function. At one time a British metropolis but at another the central representative of the Welsh people, as for example in the 2008 Eisteddfod. Probably the most important element in the second has been the location of the Welsh Assembly, which does provide a centre of Welsh government. The notion of an Assembly was once rejected and on the second occasion only just crept through, largely due to opposition from the very area where it is now located. In spite of its limitations and in a Wales among the poorest and slowest developing regions of Britain, it has become part of the life of Wales, 'an ill-favoured thing but mine own'! Even so, one has to conclude that one of the drawbacks to the strength of a Welsh identity is that it has never had a centre, a core around which to hold fast. It has been said that, 'the nature of God is a circle of which the centre is everywhere and the circumference is nowhere'; it might be said of Wales that the circumference is everywhere and the centre nowhere.

There are two problems which remain for consideration before we can review the whole problem of identity. They both arise from the nature and role of Cardiff in Wales. One is the added complexity brought into the definition of identity by the processes of recent in-migration. Indeed, in Cardiff that immigration is of long standing. It has given rise to the widely proposed concept of multiculturalism. Can one identity be formed out of many cultures? That takes us away from the notion of a developing coherence in Wales which we have put forward, to a situation of even greater diversity where presumably the move toward an integrated Welsh identity is regarded as irrelevant, or indeed to be deplored in the preferable acceptance of a composite made of different cultural groupings. Since at the very end this could lead us away from the very goal which has been taken as the purpose of this analysis, it is necessary to look at multiculturalism as a topic in itself. The second is the impact of globalisation, also linked to the modification of indigenous culture and again where the greatest impact is felt in the largest city.

Chapter 12
Multiculturalism and globalisation

In Chapter 6 the divergence between movements concerned with the recognition of Welsh identity and the growing socialist movement was discussed. As we suggested there, the language of Socialism was English and labour supporters were marked by an internationalism and a rejection of what was seen as parochial and irrelevant to the cause of the workers of the world; a side-issue of little importance. That situation has continued to the present and the great figures of the labour movement who were born in Wales have not been noted for their close association with things Welsh. Two examples can be cited. Former Welsh Secretary, George Thomas, was actively dismissive of Welshness and a firm opponent of any form of devolution. So, too, in the latter case, was Aneurin Bevan. In Michael Foot's two volume biography of Bevan the entry 'Wales' does not appear in the index.

This attitude recurs repeatedly in left orientated writings. It is worth citing an example that neatly epitomises the two views. The editor of the journal *Contemporary Wales* asked academics of differing backgrounds to review the book of essays, *'Postcolonial Wales'*, edited by Jane Aaron and Chris Williams. Professor Dai Smith neatly encapsulates the attitude of the political left. He is especially critical of Dylan Phillips's chapter on the language which dares to suggest that the language is a basic criterion of being Welsh. Indeed, the only chapter to gain any approbation is the one on migration. Smith quotes a section of it, putting a rhetorical question, 'Can we re-imagine Wales as consisting of a plurality of experiences, cultures and identities?' and adds, 'if we choose to do so, it will need to be rather more than offering the piously raised arms of the "anyone can be Welsh if they want to be variety" so beloved of politicians, largely white and recent middle-class incomers, and subscribers to Dylan Phillips's outmoded mantra of belief that: What the assembly needs to bear in mind is the fact that although 2.2 million people in Wales....are unable to speak the language, they remain Welsh [grateful thanks]. The very existence of Welsh...is the one remaining factor that identifies them as such – a people [mmm]. On the contrary, we should open up the editors' plea for further avenues of investigation by removing the shackles of a fixed Wales' (Smith, 2007, 281). This restates the issues raised in the last paragraph of the last chapter. But we hear in this the authentic voice of the long standing socialist reaction to the identification of being Welsh with the traditional cultural bases. Note the characteristic reference to 'middle class' and 'white'.

Of course, the same process has developed in England since the country has been faced with a significant immigrant population. A response parallel to that of Smith in his review has been widespread. Accusations are made that traditional definitions of things English are reliant on attitudes which are 'middle class' and 'white' and an appeal is made to a plurality of cultures or, in the more widespread form, to a 'multiculturalism'. It becomes necessary therefore to review this concept of multiculturalism in the light of the discussion which we have so far undertaken. The concept is generally propounded by the liberal left. Uncritically accepted it celebrates a benign toleration. It can be compared with a religious equivalent of 'common humanity'. The latter is a truism no one can deny but the real wealth of that humanity lies in its great variety of cultural conditions, and on their glory not on their denial. There are in humanity 'multi-cultures'. It is to these, therefore, our attention must turn.

One of the most straightforward exemplifications of a multicultural situation was apartheid South Africa. There, at least in theory, the constituent cultures of the Union were to be allowed to develop in their own ways but side by side. True it was characterised by a legal and authoritarian regime in the hands of a dominant minority - side by side meant apart and the access to resources by the various groups was grossly uneven. Nevertheless, in theory it was the complete demonstration of multiculturalism in action. At the heart of the system was segregation, and the most common form of segregation in modern times has been the ghetto. A review of its history will, therefore, give some insight into the operation of multiculturalism.

The concentration, segregation and isolation of population groups within the city have been characteristic from earliest times. From the outset cities were meeting places and by virtue of that role assembled people of different cultural backgrounds. Once lodged within the city such populations, distinctive either by their cultural practices or by their physical appearance, and frequently by both, tended to keep together, for spatial concentration maximised security in an alien environment as well as providing the most effective means of retaining identity and maintaining traditional customs, some of which demanded buildings to which access had to be immediate. But there was always a darker side in that indigenous populations fearing incomers from both economic and cultural motivations sought to isolate immigrant populations and either by custom or law to contain them within prescribed limits within the city.

This isolation of culturally alien people always generated ambivalent reactions for it has never been clear whether those discriminated against sought to retain their separate identity or wished to merge as rapidly as possible with the host population. It is a dilemma which faces all such groups. The black person, or Afro-American, in the USA is caught between regarding the ghetto or the ethnic segregation which exists as a temporary phase in an historic process that will eventually result in diffusion throughout and integration with American society, or as a means by which a different way of life can be preserved, one based on a value system different from that of White Anglo-Saxon Protestant America. It is epitomised in the demand for the use of the term Afro-American, which stresses cultural rather than physical difference. But if such contrasts are to become pivotal, it is difficult to envisage how they can operate on a non-spatial basis since different cultures use space in different ways and have habits and usages which are incompatible. Territory, as we have seen in Chapter 3 becomes critical and the ghetto, or segregation, becomes permanent.

The ghetto can play two opposite roles. The first of these is the temporary ghetto, a segregated area through which immigrant populations become adjusted to the new way of life in the host country. In particular, immigrants to a country find immediate refuge with their own kind. Then with a rise in their socio-economic status and the acquisition of native mores they become diffused throughout the host population and the ghetto disappears. An excellent example has been provided by Jakle and Wheeler (1969) in a study of Dutch immigrants into the city of Kalamazoo. In this case the immigrants were less concerned with retaining their Dutch identity than with becoming true Americans. A series of maps shows the Dutch population, identified by Dutch surnames, between 1910 and 1965. The major Dutch immigration into Kalamazoo occurred in the late nineteenth century and by 1910 clear concentrations were identifiable and remained so until 1929. By that time two distinctive Dutch clusters had appeared, one to the north and the other to the south of the city centre. Here were located what can loosely be called Dutch ghettos. They were closely associated with Dutch Churches, the crucial buildings, the pivots, about which identity was preserved. But by 1965 complete dispersion had occurred, although there was one relict concentration to the north of the central business district. The Dutch had become completely assimilated into the city and were American in all ways. The names only remained as evidence of origin.

In contrast with the above is the permanent ghetto, although the contrast is often one of degree rather than of nature. It is the means by which a cultural group can actively resist being weakened and lost in the larger community of which it has become a part. In this case the ghetto does not aid assimilation by being a stage in the process but quite the reverse. It is a means by which assimilation can be resisted and identity preserved. It must be added that the whole system can work in a contrary fashion. Where the host population actively resents the intrusion of people of different ways and customs it can take active steps to enforce the integrity of the ghetto by preventing dispersion and assimilation. That was the situation under apartheid in South Africa. It was also, in part, the condition of Jewish people in much of pre-modern Europe. The segregation of Jews was to some extent not solely the result of external pressure on 'a peculiar people' but due to the needs arising from their own religious customs, particularly the way food was prepared, the demands of attendance at a synagogue, and the need to take part in various aspects of communal life. The Jews, however, became subject to harsh, legalised conditions which institutionalised the ghetto. (The name is usually ascribed to the Ghetto Nuovo in Venice, the new foundry in Veneto, to which the Jews were restricted in 1516.) Industrialisation in the nineteenth century, allied to the movement of Jews from Eastern Europe, created ghettos in many large European cities. The best known was perhaps that in Frankfurt-on-Main established in 1462 when the Judengasse, a specially constructed street, was enclosed by walls and entered by gates, forming a clearly defined and discrete part of the city. It was not until 1798 that the prohibition that maintained the ghetto was lifted. The most infamous was the Warsaw ghetto destroyed in face of the Russian advance by the Germans in 1943. Although anti-Semitism is by no means extinct, Jews have now become completely integrated into European populations. Likewise, the enforced segregation which characterised the towns of South Africa has been dismantled, although the inheritance still lives on in parts such as Soweto.

This discussion of the ghetto may seem to have taken our investigation far from its proper track but that is not so. In the operation of the ghetto lies the key to the role of multiculturalism. Population movements, migrations, have from time immemorial characterised human society. The crux of their nature lies in the attitudes of the incomer. Presumably, and properly, and aside from violent conquest, the motivation for moving into the terrain of a different people implies the desire to become part of that people's way of life; otherwise why move? Anything else is surely unacceptable, indeed arrogant, on a par with conquest, a take over. That was the attitude of much of European colonisation in the nineteenth century which has so widely and universally been condemned. The British in India, for example, maintained a clear separation from 'the native', 'the lesser breeds without the law', and attempted to set up a British way of life in an alien territory. A whole vocabulary arose in consequence with the 'Civil Lines' and 'cantonment' well separated from the native city. That was multiculturalism in full bloom. To integrate was 'to go native'. It has been rightly reviled. But presumably it was a process of occupation rather than migration. That, of course, was the condition in medieval Wales. The Anglo-Norman occupiers established what were, in essence, ghettos. Those were the walled towns within which, isolated and protected, their own ways, customs and habits could be effectively protected.

The problem with immigration is that adaptation and integration take a considerable time and that in the first instance immigrant populations will gather together for the reasons already outlined, above all security in an alien environment, witness the Dutch in Kalamazoo. It takes at best a generation, generally more than one. This indeed was the process we traced at the outset, in Chapter 1, in relation to my own 'identity'. More generally, during that period the situation which is now labelled multiculturalism appears. I could well argue that my mother demonstrated elements of multiculturalism. Although a generation away from her English grandfather she still demonstrated some element of that English inheritance. The crucial issue is that such a condition is one in a process of transition, in spatial terms that of the temporary ghetto where a process of adaptation and integration takes place. Inevitably, there will be conflict in two ways. There will be generational conflict within the immigrant population as the younger, possibly knowing nothing of the original homeland, take on the ways of the host people. And there will be inter-ethnic conflict between the newcomers, with their alien ways, and the host population, which may find them strange and possibly objectionable. In the process of interaction cultural traits will be exchanged; the Indians play cricket, the British eat curries. But the greatest danger lies in the stalling of the integration process for segregation then becomes permanent and two often incompatible life styles exist in shared space. That is the cause of the bulk of contemporary conflict across the world, which was examined in Chapter 3. The relevance for Wales lies in the proposition that the country should always welcome the incomer who brings new ideas and innovation into the way of life, but at the same time the incomer must set out to become integrated into that culture and not set apart from it. Cultures, as we have stressed before, are not set in stone, they change and even mutate over time but they retain a basic integrity that demands respect.

One of the most sustained attacks on multiculturalism is made in the book '*The Poverty of Multiculturalism*' (2005) by Patrick West. There are obviously some elements in common between the critique which I have set out and the material in West's book but he adopts a somewhat different basis, one which is more slanted to the problems of contemporary England. That basis is contained in the proposition that western society has lost its self-confidence, defers to external criticisms and is associated with cultural relativism. 'Cultural relativism, the philosophy that no culture is superior to another, is one of today's widely accepted doctrines. In the twenty-first century, to assert the superiority of western civilisation over any other culture elicits accusations of eurocentricism, arrogance or even racism' (West, 2005, 1). The critique of this view is developed over the whole book, especially denigrating the attempts made in Britain to accommodate the cultural traits of immigrants and the willingness to modify indigenous usages. As one of many examples West quotes the exemption of Sikh motorcyclists from wearing helmets and their permission to carry ritual knives as well as all the changes made by local authorities to offset immigrant sensitivities, such as the repackaging of Christian festivals. Perhaps West would take the greatest exception to a late happening, the apparent abandonment by Random House in 2009 of the publication of '*The Jewel of Medina*' a novel by Sherry Jones on the apparent grounds that it might upset Moslem feelings. Censorship is now seemingly exercised by Moslems in western society.

West's thesis seems to depend on the contrast between what he calls universalism and cultural particularism. He quotes Johann Gottfried Herder as contending 'that man was shaped entirely by his culture, and, in particular, his language, and continues, as Isaiah Berlin elaborated, "whereas Voltaire and Diderot believed that reality was ordered in terms of universal, timeless, objective, unalterable laws which rational investigation could discover, Herder maintained that every activity, situation, historical period of civilisation possessed a unique character of its own", what Herder called a *Volksgeit*' (West, 2005, 12). It will be apparent that the opinion developed in this chapter has been much more in line with the views of Herder. Indeed, West runs into a problem in his arguments. It is illogical to equate western culture with these universal propositions. To argue, for example, that English culture is somehow a thing universal while every other culture is not is absurd. English culture is as particular in its essence as any other. What I have maintained is the particularisms of one indigenous culture should be fairly maintained against the incursions of others and not because they are superior, which is the argument West adopts, but simply because they are different.

It must be admitted that the position I have maintained is not without its own problems. If all cultures are to be seen as above judgement, a whole series of customs that are thought abhorrent to western eyes have to be accepted – female mutilation, forced marriages, honour killings, even cannibalism; the list is unending. Rejection of West's thesis is itself open to criticism. This lies at the heart of the contradiction within western liberal attitudes where any notion of the superiority of western values is rejected; it is, indeed, regarded as 'racist' and, of course, does have redolence with Nazi concepts of 'Aryan' superiority. But at the same time there is revulsion (and one can argue that such an emotion itself is not absolute but culturally derived) at many of the customs and usages which are part of other cultures. The most obvious and manifest is the treatment of women. The stoning of 'a woman caught in adultery' is not easily accepted. And it is from the import of alien customs with immigration that so many problems arise. The crucial question becomes at what point an introduced custom becomes unacceptable in a new environment.

What I have maintained in this chapter and throughout the book is that an indigenous culture has to be respected by immigrants, that by the very nature of their incoming they have to accept the mores of the host country, anything else is either in the form of conquest or is unacceptable arrogance. And the host country has no obligation to adapt its ways to accommodate the incomers. On the other hand, no culture is immutable, its nature will change over time and some of that change will be due to the impact of other people with other ways.

At this stage it is appropriate to turn to the less physically tangible but possibly greater impact of globalization. It is a truism, but none the less valid for that, that the great protector of cultural integrity is isolation. From time to time the media have been greatly taken with the discovery in the remotest of tropical forests of tribes found in isolation, and hence maintaining usages and customs untrammelled by the outside world. A great load of meaning is carried by that expression 'outside world' for external influences bear heavily upon identity differentials. Critically, since the end of the Second World War, isolation has been progressively shattered, not only by easier physical movement over the longest of distances but by electronic devices. Films, distributed world wide, access to radio and television, the internet, indeed the whole range of media, have tended to erode regional differences and promote the universal. It was, of course, to counter those threats that the demand for a Welsh television channel arose to parallel BBC Radio Cymru. The recent attempt to set up a Welsh language daily paper, which failed for lack of Government support, is an acknowledgement of the significance of the media. There is no doubt that globalisation diminishes the differences between peoples and produces a less diversified world.

It will be evident that although reference was made earlier to folk culture and its modern translation into 'pop', little discussion of its relevance has been offered. It is in this area of globalization that it becomes most important. In the realms of jazz, rock and roll and all the innumerable variation of popular music, it would be difficult to identity a distinctive Welsh form. The Super Furry Animals, a successful band formed in Cardiff in 1993, have produced a Welsh language disc but the endeavour of most such artists is to 'get into the charts', to be 'top of the pops', 'to break into the American market', and to be global in reach rather than produce something so identifiable and distinctively Welsh that its broader market would be lost. What all this means is that the greater threat to identity comes not necessarily from immigration but from the insidious reach of external ways. Of those centres exporting different ways, the USA is by far the most powerful, by virtue of its economic strength and the depth of its market. It is little wonder that it is so feared and in some cases reviled by peoples across the world who wish to preserve ways of life based on different principles.

At the end of this review, therefore, it is possible to argue that the greatest factor in the modification of indigenous ways of life comes not from the movement of populations, significant as they are, but from external influences which show every sign of becoming more far reaching and more powerful with time and technical advance.

Chapter 13

The Welsh identity:
a summation

At the end of chapter 11 we used the simile that if Welsh identity could be conceived as a circle the centre was nowhere and the circumference everywhere. It is somewhat fanciful but contains a kernel of truth. The basic and central elements which constitute the being of a people, the laws, customs, rites and usages, were ripped out and quite deliberately and cynically obliterated by the Edwardian conquest and the preceding and succeeding Anglo-Norman occupation. What was left was destroyed by an Act of Union designed to remove all 'the sinister usages and customs differing' from those of the English. Marc Morris in his book on Edward I quotes an English clerk writing in Rome in 1283 on the death of Llewelyn ap Gruffudd, 'Glory be to God in the highest, peace on earth to men of good will, a triumph to the English, victory to King Edward, honour to the church, rejoicing to the Christian faith, confusion to jealous men, dismay to envious ones, and to the Welsh everlasting extermination' (Morris, 2008, 187). Although extermination was not achieved, after the Act of Union little was left of the old Welsh way of life, especially in its more formal aspects.

What did survive, in spite of the attempts at elimination, was the language and the culture that the literature in that language enshrined. But that was itself only partial for the language was eradicated from much of the marcher territory so that, tragically, instead of becoming both the cement and symbol of unity, it became a source of difference separating the Welsh from the Welsh. The Assembly Government hopefully looks to '*Iaith Pawb*' (2003), *Welsh as a Language for All*, but that objective is a good way off. In that sense, therefore, as in all others, as Chapter 11 showed, there has never been a centre, a nucleus, either actual or immaterial for the Welsh people. Instead, there has been a whole series of different contexts of being Welsh floating around the wheel of a circumference, an airy nothing lacking a local habitation and a name. Certainly, other peoples demonstrate variations on a theme, for example there are clear differences between a Geordie and a Cockney, but they are somehow not as fundamental as those that affect the Welsh, which is possibly why the Welsh have been so eminently concerned with their identity. Paradoxically, however, within the series of varying interpretations two can be isolated as the predominant themes, or positions, on which that identity is based.

The first of these positions is that of the Welsh speakers well versed in the literary and cultural traditions of the country and who maintain that the language is the prime definer of ethnic identity, and that the only true Welshman or woman is a Welsh speaker. Those outside this circle can only claim to be Welsh in a modified fashion, for their unwillingness to learn and use the language is symbolic of a critical failure of will and a signifier of a lack of intent to be properly Welsh. Three points must be made in relation to this position. The first is that there is a danger that in constant reference to the language it can become conceived as a thing in itself almost akin to a set of mathematical characters. But language is very different in that it carries a rich depth of historical and cultural associations and it is for that complex that language stands as a surrogate. The second aspect of that position is that by no means all Welsh speakers of necessity adopt it. There are Welsh speakers who regard the language as an unnecessary qualifier of the Welsh identity and, indeed, one that by its exclusive character sadly depletes the inclusive nature of the Welsh people. An associated third aspect is indicated by the 2001 census where only 14.4 per cent actually wrote themselves in as Welsh, a proportion below that of Welsh speakers at 18.7 per cent. Presumably, those who refused to complete the census are not counted so that the implication is that some Welsh speakers either did not want to declare themselves as Welsh or were ignorant of the possibilities of doing so. Either way it reflects on the total commitment of some Welsh speakers to the position outlined above.

The second position is that of non Welsh-speakers who even so regard themselves as thoroughly and truly Welsh and reject the language as the sole or even main definer of character. Identity in this case has been an intangible association with location, though more recently built around the range of civil or national institutions which have been developed in Wales over the past hundred years. These institutions are in many ways a restitution, a recreation, of those aspects of identity which had been destroyed by the Anglo-Norman conquest and all the consequent processes which made it possible to write 'for Wales, see England'. This attitude has been effectively summarised by Merfyn Jones. 'The Welsh are in the process of being defined, not in terms of shared occupational experience or common religious inheritance or the survival of an ancient European language or for contributing to the Welsh radical tradition, but rather by reference to the institutions that they inhabit, influence, and react to. This new identity may lack the ethical and political imperatives that characterised Welsh life for two centuries but it increasingly looks like the only identity available' (M. Jones, 1992, 356). Since that was written a new and powerful nucleus has been given to that 'new identity' by the creation of the Welsh

Assembly, for the range of policies which the Assembly has developed emphasise difference and promote separation. Even so, the manifest hesitation over the holding of a referendum on further powers for the Assembly suggests a certain lack of conviction over this central role.

It is, therefore, sensible to recognise that this institutionally-based identity is neither totally secure nor homogeneous. Within it on the one hand are those who have a warm feeling for the language and the culture it embodies, while on the other there are those who regard the language and all its associations as outmoded and a hindrance to a general feeling of togetherness that should be at the heart of Welshness; the language is a divider inherited from the past and best forgotten. These are two extremes and in reality there is every nuance between them.

It is possible to add a third position to the two proposed. There are those who are Welsh in the sense of having been born in the country and are not first generation immigrants, but have little feeling of association with things Welsh. They are tacitly Welsh for they can claim no other association, but avoid embracing that identity. The way out is to declare themselves British. There is in this a little of the nineteenth century attitude that being Welsh has something of the lesser breeds without the law, something to which one would not readily admit in polite society!

There is one element that detaches this last group from many in the others, except perhaps the less committed part of the second group. This is attitude to the monarchy. The Crown is seen by that section of the population, as in England, as a symbol of identity, part of the core, to which it gives unity and meaning. It is difficult without evidence to assign attitudes to a majority of Welsh people but certainly by some the monarchy is generally regarded as an anachronism having nothing whatsoever to do with Wales. One has to sympathise with the Prince of Wales's enforced efforts to demonstrate an interest in the country when the very title he holds is regarded by many as an insult to the Welsh people. At least some will disagree with that sentence. Once again, the sorts of institutions which could give strength to being Welsh are just as divisive.

It is possible to add yet another element to the complex of attitudes which have been outlined, one that is characteristic of the late twentieth and the twenty first centuries. This is the so-called 'cool Cymru', a description that comes up in the press from time to time and purports to represent more effectively a contemporary Wales. It is, of course the application of the cult of personality to things Welsh and an attempt to establish an identity in association with the 'celebrities' of the day. It is a sort of 'Hello' or 'OK' magazine aspect of being Welsh. An article by Steffan Rhys in the Western Mail for May 30, 2008, presents a lengthy list of people or places that have obtained a degree of fame, from *Gavin and Stacey* to the Hay Literary Festival. To rehearse them all would be more plagiarism than quotation. It is indicative that when BBC Wales made a programme on 'Welsh Greats' the first in the series was not Llewelyn ap Gruffudd or Owain Glyn Dŵr, or even Gwynfor Evans, but Richard Burton. This contemporary cult of personality is far removed from the discussions which have taken place in this book but it cannot be ignored for it does provide a core of common feeling for some, however trivial the context. I have often wondered why Welsh boys, and indeed adults, declare themselves to be fanatical supporters of Manchester United, or Liverpool for that matter. As Hamlet says, 'What's Hecuba to him or he to Hecuba'. Manchester United has one prominent Welsh player, Ryan Giggs, and Liverpool might be the de facto capital of north Wales, but the real reason is the need to have an association with success, with something that is 'in the news', and the world-wide news at that where Cardiff City, Swansea City, or alack Wrexham, seldom are. If the denizens of 'cool Cymru', even in their passing show, can generate a warmth of association with things Welsh, they play a role in the search for that core which could give coherence to being Welsh.

As we have contended, there are no discrete, neat polar opposites in this sense of identity that we have sought to define but rather a melange, a confused array of attitudes and positions which is, of course, the heart of the problem. Even so it is appropriate briefly to consider directions for the future which, as it were, emerge from the mists of confusion. Clearly, this has to be limited for otherwise an extensive critique of the cultural and institutional futures would carry us beyond the intentions of this volume. To some degree, with my colleague John Aitchison I have attempted this in the two books *'Language, Culture and Society. The Changing Fortunes of the Welsh Language in the Twentieth century'* and *'Spreading the Word. The Welsh Language 2001'*.

The title of the latter book summarises the trajectory of the language in recent times, for the evidence shows, if not resurgence, certainly a reversal of the long trend of decline. Moreover, there is a wide range of institutions that strongly support the language. Among these are the whole structure of Welsh medium education, the media in the form of BBC Radio Cymru and S4C and such basic providers of written material as the Welsh Books Council, along with a number of publishers, such as Gwasg Gomer and Y Lolfa. All these are backed by substantial and vocal protagonists, such as Cymdeithas Yr Iaith Gymraeg. There is no question, therefore, that the language is in a better state than it has been for many decades. But there are problems. In the past the main transmitters of language, and indeed of the culture associated with it, have been the family, or the household, and the chapel. These have lost their influence. Both census and surveys show that the use of the language within the household has diminished, while the chapel has all but disappeared as a basic element in language preservation, especially through the Sunday school. The main transmitter of language therefore has become the educational system, especially the Welsh language schools. But as Ellis and mac aGhobhain (1972) write, 'A language cannot be saved by singing a few songs or having a word on a postage stamp. It cannot even be saved by getting "official status" for it, or getting it taught in schools. It is saved by its use (no matter how imperfectly), by its introduction and use in every walk of life and at every conceivable opportunity until it becomes a natural thing, no longer laboured or false. It means in short a period of struggle and hardship. There is no easy route to the restoration of language'. And therein lies the problem. The Welsh Language Board clearly recognises this difficulty and enterprises such as 'Iaith Gwaith' are directed to offset the dominant use of English in public places – or in another campaign, 'Dechreuwch pob sgwrs yn Gymraeg'. Again, there is the problem in the background of the uncritical association of language with identity: it is not one which can be ignored for they are not of necessity entirely concomitant.

In contrast, the 'institutional' basis of identity seems to be exhibiting increased tenacity. One may perhaps regard with some scepticism the hyperbole of the Presiding Officer of the National Assembly, Lord Dafydd Elis-Thomas, – 'The new Government of Wales Act 2006 shakes the historic relationship between England and Wales to its roots…The new legal situation in Wales means that we can talk of the Welsh Statute Book, Welsh Law, and of redeveloping a body of laws which link us historically with the laws of the princes – The Law of Hywel – one of Welsh culture's most splendid creations, a powerful symbol of our unity and identity, as powerful as the Welsh language itself' (Ellis-Thomas, 2007. Address at the National Assembly, quoted in Osmond, 2008).

Without independence the creations of the Assembly are more likely to be variations on an original theme established at Westminster. However, most surveys show an increasing support for enhanced powers for the Assembly. John Osmond writes 'since the 1997 (referendum) opinion has swung emphatically in favour of establishing a Scottish-style Parliament with law-making powers...According to the latest survey, carried out in the wake of the May 2007 Assembly election, only 16 per cent are opposed to some degree of democratic self-government for Wales. Some 28 per cent support the current Assembly, and 12 per cent support independence. The important statistic, however, is that 44 per cent favour moving ahead to achieve a Scottish-style parliament' (Osmond, 2008, 16), although that is less than half of those surveyed. Some caution needs to be shown in relation to these survey data. Even so, Osmond in his consideration of 'Assembly to Senedd' has no doubts of the progress of an institutional-based identity. He writes that 'a political unity around devolution is developing in what was once a highly fractured country so far as attitudes to Welsh political aspirations are concerned. Certainly, it supports the view that there is a "settled will" on moving towards greater powers for the National Assembly' (Osmond, 2008, 22).

If this be so, one has to wonder why all those who support further powers are so reluctant to propose an immediate referendum. The creation of the All Welsh Convention to consider the future nature of the governance of Wales seems somehow concerned with the delay of a referendum in case it were lost rather than with the development of any novel means for the governance of Wales. Maybe there is the legitimate assumption, derived from all the evidence of surveys, that much of the opposition to the advance of self-government comes from the more elderly and that time will, therefore, erode opposition. But many of the old antagonisms to the independent identity of Wales that characterised much of the Labour movement have not disappeared and are represented among the population as well as among labour Members of Parliament. Merfyn Jones's conclusion, which was quoted above, was made at a time when the language was in a much less healthy state than it is now and, accordingly, it would be unwise to conclude that the language-cultural basis of identity is in a state of decline as against an advancing institutional basis. What the country needs is a rapprochement between these two bases of identity and in spite of some vociferous opposition that seems to be occurring.

From the destruction of early times we have inherited a shattered cultural core. If we refer back to Chapter 2 a whole series of cultural elements was defined but in most cultures those elements do not exist in separation, rather they are intimately related or integrated into a whole. The critical issue in Wales was the dissolution of its early culture by force majeur, a fragmentation which has generated conflict, that conflict exacerbated by a porous eastern border and the consequent patterns of immigration. The past 150 years have seen a slow and incomplete process of the reintegration of these elements of cultural identity. That process has produced the perpetual arguments over the role of the language and identity. Welsh identity is still a condition with infinite variety, not diminished by modern custom, where each person has his or her own interpretation. In that sense the work of Edward I and of the Act of Union still stand as fundamentally successful after many centuries in having robbed Wales of its coherence and unity as a people and substituted conflict and rancour.

It follows that the real task of the contemporary leaders of Welsh affairs is to promote that sense of coherence which would give so much more strength to the people's future. It is not an easy task as wrangles over the role of the language continue daily in spite of the fine rhetoric of 'Iaith Pawb' – 'A truly bilingual Wales, by which we mean a country where people can choose to live their lives through the medium of either or both Welsh or English and where the presence of the language is a source of pride' (Welsh Assembly Government, 2003, 1). Differences over the status and especially the future powers of the Assembly still exist, too. But it is a task which after centuries of division needs to be done. Moreover, with the growing strength of the Scottish National Party, as well as the rising tide of English objections to what are seen as 'provincial' advantages, it would seem that some form of a federal Britain is likely to develop in the future. In that, a separate Wales would have the chance and opportunity to forge that single identity for which this volume has searched.

References

Aitchison, J.W. and Carter, H. (1987)
The Welsh language in Cardiff: a quiet
revolution. Transactions of the Institute of
British Geographers, New Series, 12, 482-492.

Aitchison, J.W. and Carter, H. (1998)
The regeneration of the Welsh language: an
analysis. Contemporary Wales, 11, 167-185.

Aitchison, J.W. and Carter, H. (2000)
Language, Economy and Society. The
Changing Fortunes of the Welsh Language
in the Twentieth Century.

Aitchison, J.W. and Carter, H. (2004)
Spreading the Word: The Welsh Language
2001. Talybont, Y Lolfa.

Allen, J. and Mooney, E. (1998)
Migration into rural communities: questioning
the language of counter-urbanisation, in
P.Boyle and K. Halfacre edits. Migration into
Rural Areas. London, Wiley.

Anderson, B. (2006)
Imagined Communities.
London and New York, Verso.

Andersen, R. (2009)
National Identity and Independence Attitudes:
Minority Nationalism in Scotland and Wales.
Oxford, CRESS.

Armstrong, W.A. (1972)
The use of information about occupations, in
E.A. Wrigley edit. Nineteenth Century Society.
Cambridge University Press, Cambridge. Chap 6

Arnold, M. (1867)
On the Study of Celtic Literature, in The
Works of Matthew Arnold, Macmillan, London.

Balsom, D. (1995)
The Three Wales model, in Osmond J. edit.
The National Question Again. Welsh Political
Identity in the 1980s. Llandysul, Gwasg Gomer.

Bashir, H and Lewis, D. (2008)
Tears of the Desert. London, Hodder.

Beard, C. and Cerf, C. (1992)
The Officially Correct Dictionary
and Handbook. London, Graffion.

Betts, C. (1997)
Kill the language. Call by Professor.
Western Mail, January 28, 1977.

Bernstein, B. (1970)
A socio-linguistic approach to socialisation,
in J. Gumperz and D. Hymes edits.
Directions in Socio-Linguistics. New York,
Rinehart and Winston

Blackaby, D., Murphy, P., O'Leary, N.
and Thomas, E. (1995)
Wales: an economic survey. Contemporary
Wales, 8, 213-295.

Bowen, I. (1908)
Statutes of Wales. London, T Fisher Unwin.

Capstick, M. (1987)
Housing dilemmas in the Lake District.
Lancaster, Centre for North West
Regional Studies.

Carter, H. (1965)
The Towns of Wales. Cardiff, University
of Wales Press.

Carter, H. and Thomas, J.G. (1969)
The referendum on the Sunday opening of
licensed premises in Wales as a criterion of a
culture region. Regional Studies, 3, 61-71.

Carter, H. (1976)
Y Fro Gymraeg and the 1975 referendum
on the closing of public houses in Wales.
Cambria, 3, 89-101.

Carter, H. and Wheatley, S. (1982)
Merthyr Tydfil in 1851. A Study of the

Spatial Structure of a Welsh Industrial Town.
Cardiff, University of Wales Press. Social
Science Monographs No. 7.

Carter, H. (1995)
The Study of Urban Geography. 4th edit.
London, Arnold.

Carter, H. (1998)
Whose city? A view from the periphery.
Transactions of the Institute of British
Geographers, New Series, 14, 4-23.

Champion, T. (1992)
Migration processes and patterns. Vol. 1
Research Progress and Migration patterns.
London, Bellhaven Press.

Cline, E. (2009)
Biblical Archaeology: A Very Short
Introduction. Oxford, Oxford University Press.

Cloke, P., Goodwin, M. and Milbourne, P. (1995)
'There's so many strangers in the village now':
marginalisation and change in 1990s Welsh
rural life-styles. Contemporary Wales, 8, 47-74.

Daunton, M. (1978)
Towns and economic growth in eighteenth
century England, in P .A. Abrahams and E.A.
Wrigley edits. Towns and Societies. Essays in
Economic History and Historical Sociology.
Cambridge, University of Cambridge Press.

Davies, J. (1993)
A History of Wales. London, Penguin Group.

Davies, J., Jenkins, N., Baines, M. and
Lynch, P.I. (2008)
Encyclopaedia of Wales. Cardiff, University
of Wales Press.

Davies, R.R. (1978)
Brecon, in R.A. Griffiths edit. Op. Cit.

Davies, R.R. (1987)
The Age of Conquest. Wales 1063-1415.
Oxford, Oxford University Press.

Douglas, M. (2003)
Natural Symbols. Explorations in Cosmology.
London, Routledge Classics.

Edwards, H.T. (1987)
Y Cymraeg yn y bedwaredd ganrif ar
bymtheg, in G.H. Jenkins edit. Cof Cenedl 2.
Llandysul, Gwasg Gomer.

Ellis, P. and mac a'Ghobhainn. (1971)
The Problem of Language Revival. Inverness,
Club Leabhar.

Fisher, H.A.L. (1944)
A History of Europe. London, Edward Arnold.

Fishlock, T (1972)
Wales and the Welsh. London, Casell.

Giggs, J. and Pattie, C. (1992)
'Croeso I Gymru – Welcome to Wales':
but to whose Wales? Area, 24, 268-282.

Giggs, J. and Pattie, C. (1992)
Wales as a plural society. Contemporary
Wales, 5, 25-64.

Griffiths, R. (2007)
Hen Wlad fy Nhadau in its musical context.
Morgannwg, L1, 6-18

Griffiths, R.A. edit. (1978)
The Boroughs of Medieval Wales. Cardiff,
University of Wales Press.

Griffiths, W. (1968)
The Welsh. Cardiff, University of Wales Press

Henken, E.R. (1996)
National Redeemer. Owain Glyndŵr in Welsh
Tradition. Cardiff, University of Wales Press.

Huntington, S.P. (2004)
Who are We? America's Great Debate.
London, Simon and Schuster.

Jakle, J.A. and Wheeler, J.O. (1969)
The changing residential structure of the
Dutch population of Kalamazoo, Michigan.
Annals of the Association of American
Geographers, 59, 441-460.

Jefferson, M. (1939)
The law of the primate city. Geographical
Review, 29, 227.

Jenkins, G.H. (1993)
The Foundations of Modern Wales. Wales
1642-1780. Oxford, Oxford University Press.

Jones, I.G. (1976)
The Religious Census of 1858. A Calendar of
the Returns relating to Wales. Vol. 1 South
Wales. Cardiff, University of Wales Press.

Jones, I.G. (1981)
Explorations and Explanations. Essays in the
Social History of Victorian Wales. Llandysul,
Gomer Press.

Jones, I.G. (1992)
Mid Victorian Wales. The Observers and the
Observed. Cardiff, University of Wales Press.

Jones, M. (1992)
Beyond Identity? The reconstruction of the
Welsh. The Journal of British Studies, 31,4.

Kroeber, A.L. and Cluckhohn C. (1952)
Culture. A Critical review of Concepts and
Definitions. Papers of the Peabody Museum
of American Archaeology and Ethnology, Vol.
XLVII-No.1 Cambridge, Mass.

Lang, G.E. and Lang, K. (1983)
The Battle for Public Opinion. The President,
Press and the Polls during Watergate.
New York, Columbia University Press.

Levi-Strauss, C. (1997)
Structural Anthropology. Trans. Monique
Layton. London, Allen Lane.

Ley, D. and Cybriwsky, R. (1974)
Urban graffiti as territorial markers. Annals of
the Association of American Geographers, 64,
491-505.

Little, L.K and Rosenwein, B.H. edits. (1998)
Debating the Middle Ages. Oxford, Blackwell.

Livingstone, A.G., Spears, R. and
Manstead, S.R. (2009)
The language of change? Characterisations
of ingroup social position, threat, and the
deployment of "distinctive" group attitudes.
Cardiff, SISAW.

Mandelbaum, D.G. (1949)
Selected Writings of Edward Sapir. Berkeley,
Calif. University of California Press.

McCombs, M. and Shaw, D. (1972)
The agenda setting function of the mass
media. Opinion Quarterly, 36, 176-187.

Medhurst, K. (1982)
Basques and Basque nationalism, in
C.Williams edit. National Separatism. 235-
262. Cardiff, University of Wales Press.

Mitchell, D. (1995)
There is no such thing as culture: towards a
reconceptualisation of the idea of culture in
geography. Transactions of the Institute of
British Geographers, New Series, 20, 102-116.

Morgan, K.O. (1981)
The Rebirth of a Nation. Wales 1880-1980.
Oxford, Clarendon Press.

Morris, M. (2008)
A Great and Terrible King. Edward the
First and the Forging of Britain. London,
Hutchinson.

National Assembly for Wales (2002)
Our Language: Its Future. Policy Review of
the Welsh Language. Cardiff, Culture
Committee and Education and Lifelong
Learning Committee.

National Assembly for Wales, Statistical
Directorate. (2005)
Second Homes in Wales,2005. A Comparison
of the sources of data about second homes in
Wales. Cardiff, Welsh Assembly Government.

National Assembly for Wales. Statistical
Directorate. (2006)
Patterns of Migration in Wales. Cardiff, Welsh
Assembly Government.

National Statistical Office (2008)
Wales. Its People. London, HMSO.

Naval Intelligence Division (1944)
Belgium. Geographical Handbook Series.

Naval Intelligence Division (1944)
Jugoslavia. Geographical Handbook Series.

Nelde, P., Strubell, M. and Williams, G. (1996)
The Production and Reproduction of the
Minority Language Groups in the European
Union. Luxembourg, Office for the Official
Publications of the European Union.

O Siochru, M. (2008)
God's Executioner. Oliver Cromwell and the
Conquest of Ireland. London, Faber.

Office of National Statistics. Labour Force
Survey (LFS), a quarterly sample survey of
households living at private addresses in Great
Britain that provides information on the UK
labour market.

Osmond, J. (2008)
Assembly to Senedd. The Convention and
the move to legislative powers. Cardiff,
The Institute of Welsh affairs.

Owen, T.M. (1991)
The Customs and Traditions of Wales.
Cardiff, University of Wales Press.

Parliamentary Papers (1881)
CCLX,1748-1778.

Paxman, J. (1999)
The English. A Portrait of a People.
London, Penguin Books.

Pohl, W. (1998)
Concepts of ethnicity in early Medieval
studies. In Little and Rosenwein edits.
Debating the Middle Ages. 15-24.

Prunier, G. (2009)
From Genocide to Continental War. The
Congolese Conflict and the Crisis of
Contemporary Africa. London, Hurst and Co.

Pryce, W.T.R. (2006)
Region or national territory? Regionalism and
the idea of the country of Wales. The Welsh
History Review, 23, 99-152

Roberts, G.T. (1998)
The Language of the Blue Books. Cardiff,
University of Wales Press

Rowley, G. (1984)
Israel into Palestine. London and New York,
Mansell.

Sand, S. (2009)
The Invention of the Jewish People.
London, Verso

Sanghera, S. (2008)
If You Don't Know Me by Now. A Memoir
of Love, Secrets and Lies in Wolverhampton.
London, Viking.

Sinclair, A. (1962)
Prohibition. The Era of Excess.
London, Faber

Smith, D. (2007)
Wales: Post in Parenthesis, in Review
Symposium: Postcolonial Wales.
Contemporary Wales, 19, 276-283.

Smith, A.D. (1986)
The Ethnic Origins of Nations.
Oxford, Blackwell.

Smith, R. (1999)
Aberystwyth, in G.Parry a M.A.Williams edits.
Miliwn o Gymry Gymraeg! Yr Iaith Gymraeg
a Chyfryfiad 1891. Caerdydd, Gwasg
Prifysgol Cymru.

Stevens, C. (1996)
Meithrin. Hanes Mudiad Ysgolion Meithrin.
Llandysul, Gwasg Gomer

Stillwell, J. Rees, P. and Boden, P. (1992)
Migration Processes and Patterns. Population
Redistribution in the 1980s. Vol 2.
London, Bellhaven Press.

Thomas, B. (1987)
A Cauldron, a Rebirth. Population and the
Welsh Language in the Nineteenth Century.
Welsh History Review, 13, 418-437.

Tudur, G. (1989)
Wyt Ti'n Cofio? Chwarter Canrif o Frwydr
yr Iaith. Talybont, Y Lolfa.

Welsh Assembly Government (2003)
Iaith Pawb. A National Action Plan for a
Bilingual Wales. Cardiff, WAG.

Welsh Language Board (1996)
A Strategy for the Welsh Language. Cardiff

West, P. (2005)
The Poverty of Multiculturalism.
London, Civitas.

Wickham, C. (2009)
The Inheritance of Rome. A History of
Europe from 400 to 1000. London,
Allen Lane.

Williams, D. (1950)
A History of Modern Wales.
London, John Murray.

Williams, Glanmor. (1993)
Renewal and Reformation. Wales 1415-1642.
Oxford, Oxford University Press.

Williams, G.A. (1979)
When was Wales? London, BBC.

Williams, G.A. (1966)
The Merthyr of Dic Penderyn, in G.A.
Williams edit. Merthyr Politics: The Making
of a Working Class Tradition.
Cardiff, University of Wales Press.

Williams, G.A. (1978)
The Merthyr Rising. London, Croomhelm.

Williams, Glyn. (1986)
Recent trends in the sociology of Wales,
in I. Hulme and W.T.R. Pryce edits.
The Welsh and Their Country. 176-194.
Llandysul, Gomer Press.

Williams-Jones, K. (1978)
Caernarfon, in R.A. Griffiths, Op Cit.72-101.

Wilson, W.J. (1978)
The Declining Significance of Race. Blacks
and Changing American Institutions.
Chicago, University of Chicago Press.

Wuthnow, R. et al. (1984)
Cultural Analysis. Boston, Routledge
and Kegan Paul.